The Entrepreneur's Guide to Successful Leadership

**Recent Titles in
The Entrepreneur's Guide**

The Entrepreneur's Guide

CJ Rhoads, Series Editor

The Entrepreneur's Guide to Successful Leadership

Dan Goldberg and Don Martin

Westport, Connecticut
London

Library of Congress Cataloging-in-Publication Data

Goldberg, Dan, 1947–
    The entrepreneur's guide to successful leadership / Dan Goldberg and Don Martin.
        p. cm.—(The entrepreneur's guide, ISSN 1939–2478)
    Includes bibliographical references and index.
    ISBN 978–0–313–35288–1 (alk. paper)
    1. Leadership. 2. Entrepreneurship. 3. Success in business. 4. Small
business—Management. I. Martin, Don, 1943– II. Title.
    HD57.7.G6638 2008
    658.4'092—dc22   2008028220

British Library Cataloguing in Publication Data is available.

Library of Congress Catalog Card Number: 2008028220
ISBN: 978–0–313–35288–1
ISSN: 1939–2478

First published in 2008

Praeger Publishers, 88 Post Road West, Westport, CT 06881
An imprint of Greenwood Publishing Group, Inc.
www.praeger.com

Printed in the United States of America

∞™

The paper used in this book complies with the
Permanent Paper Standard issued by the National
Information Standards Organization (Z39.48–1984).

10 9 8 7 6 5 4 3 2 1

We dedicate this book to all the past, present, and future entrepreneurial leaders.

Contents

Preface

Leadership is a skill that can take ordinary situations, businesses, organizations, and individuals into the realm of the extraordinary. As we pondered the attributes necessary for would-be and current entrepreneurs to take their ideas and ventures into the reality of success, we examined our pasts, the stories of others, and additional available resources to make the journey toward your desires as smooth and relevant as possible.

While writing this book we thought of you, our readers, and how you would want to have the elements of successful entrepreneurial leadership delivered. We discovered that relating the experiences of ourselves and others would make for an interesting guide, one based on real events that help illustrate the steps necessary to build profitable ventures out of embryonic thoughts, creative ideas, underdeveloped market niches, and just plain entrepreneurial desire.

As we constructed this book, we recognized the need for ease in following each of the steps in our Entrepreneurial Leadership Model. By using concise illustrations, simple tools, short assessments, key points, and lessons learned, we strove to make your trip into entrepreneurial leadership as easy as possible. We have also given you additional resources to help speed your journey along. As you check out our resources, including books, magazines, and Websites, you will find insightful elements that will tie into what you will read within the pages of this book.

By coupling the skills, learning resources, words, and other ingredients contained in this volume, you will receive valuable and immediately usable information to help you start or build your business.

Being entrepreneurs ourselves, we've seen and have been involved in many of the joys and disappointments that have, or may, face you in your endeavors. Although both of us continue to sail the waters of the seas of entrepreneurship, we also have the added resources of the academic world. Each of us is involved in teaching businesspeople, including those already established and others who are just entering a new venture, in the processes necessary to turn entrepreneurial dreams into reality.

While we work with people in university settings, as well as corporate locations, we gain further insights into the ongoing needs of the entrepreneur. With technology making the pace of decisions, transitions, information, and other aspects of business faster and more transparent, today's entrepreneurial leader needs every possible edge.

By developing a leadership model to assist you, we have taken each step and broken it into easily digestible pieces. Starting with the foundation of entrepreneurship and moving you up to success, we have taken into account how you, as a leader, should function within the day-to-day reality of the business world.

Incorporated within the pages of this book are real-life situations that help you understand what entrepreneurs go through as they strive for success.

Whether you are a well-seasoned business owner or a novice, you can use the advice we've spelled out to help you over some of the hurdles you may be facing, or lead you in a new direction. In some cases you may find that the business you think you'd like to start may not be the most viable venture.

When you take our assessments, you may realize certain aspects of your behavior, motivations, and value system that may be better suited for something new, old, or different. Our purpose in writing *The Entrepreneur's Guide to Successful Leadership* is to not only give you useful tips, advice, and knowledge, but also to help you realize certain talents hidden inside that can blossom in ways you may never have dreamed.

Acknowledgments

Our sincerest thanks to all the people who helped make this book and our entrepreneurial experiences possible. Although we'd like to list each one of them individually, there are far too many folks who have touched our lives to mention each one by name.

However, the following people stand out in their help and guidance in the formation of this book. Bud Batcher, our partner in the Institute for Effective Leadership and good friend, who diligently edited our first draft and added his insights as Key Points and Lessons Learned at the end of each chapter. We are fortunate to have Bud on our team. He is our golf coach and the third leg of what we call the Don, Dan, and Bud "360s"—three guys in their sixties who have holistic perspectives.

Sue, Don's wife and truly his "better half," whose help, understanding, and feedback during his entrepreneurial years and the writing of this book has added to the depth and texture of so many of his experiences. Chadd, their son, is a successful entrepreneur in his own right. Chadd and his wife, Mandy, and their two children, Owen and Abigail, will be the next generation of Martin entrepreneurs. Daughter Becky is an inspiration and gives them much pride as a second-degree black belt. She is a source of joy in their life.

Don's father, Louis, taught him how to work with people, and his mother, Carolyn, taught him to never give up and to love books. Don's brother, Rich, and his two sisters, Carol and Deb, each continue to inspire him.

Reni Goldberg, Dan's son. His opinions, thoughts, and ideas help to keep his dad on track and cognizant of the broadest elements in our global society; his humor, intelligence, and unconditional love are priceless. Other major players in Dan's entrepreneurial leadership journey include his mother, Frances, whose knowledge, guidance, and love keep him on course; brother, Jack; sister-in-law, Jane; daughter-in-law, Sonia; aunt, Toby; and close friends, Ron Goldberg and Cindy Clair, David and Myrna Ginsberg, Howard and Denise Stredler, and Bill and Donna Miller. Their constant support, insight, and camaraderie cannot be adequately expressed in words.

Dan's father, Ralph, who started him on his entrepreneurial endeavors and was his mentor and guide in so many aspects of life, his son, Marcus, and daughter Reyna; though each of them has left this earth, they still are part of the fabric of his life and continue to provide him with constant motivation.

Our friends and colleagues at Kutztown University of Pennsylvania, Temple University, and Penn State University for their encouragement and fellowship; in particular, Christine "CJ" Rhoads, entrepreneur, Kutztown University associate professor and *Entrepreneur's Guide* series editor, who brought us the opportunity to write this book and worked with us throughout its development. Her editing skills and guidance were invaluable. Jeff Olson, senior acquisitions editor at Praeger Publishers and Rebecca Edwards, senior project manager at Cadmus Communications—their help in bringing this project to fruition was invaluable. Andrea Lewis of the Kutztown Small Business Development Center coordinated the final editing of the book and the construction of the index. Also, Heather A. Mayer, of Kutztown University, assisted us in the writing of the learning resources appendix.

Catherine Nemetz of Envisions created the graphics in this book. Her work is always like "magic." We thank her for her continued support of our business.

Ernie Post, Director, Kutztown University Small Business Development Center (SBDC), Peter Hornberger, and Lenin Agudo are integral parts of the same SBDC. All three have given their knowledge, support, and skills to entrepreneurs for years.

And, to our clients, who inspire us daily.

Introduction: The Entrepreneurial Challenge

Like you, we are entrepreneurs—people with business dreams who work hard to fulfill them. We know that to stand above the crowded field, tenacity, passion, drive, and a workable leadership model for success can give a businessperson an advantage in the entrepreneurial landscape.

The word *entrepreneur* has become a catch-all title for just about everyone who starts and/or builds a small business.

Is an entrepreneur someone who takes the family business and keeps it going? Is it the person who builds a new division of the company where he or she is employed? Or should it be reserved for only those who have put everything on the line to build their business? To us, it doesn't matter. In this book, we will concentrate on advice for all of the above-mentioned groups. Because entrepreneurs come in a number of different varieties and share some measure of risk, our guide should help any entrepreneur see things with a bit more clarity.

At an area Chamber of Commerce awards dinner some years back, the recipient of the entrepreneur of the year award went to a gentleman whose father had started the business many years before and built it into quite a successful venture. By the time the son had arrived to run the company, it was already a multimillion-dollar operation. However, the enormous growth created by the son made him, in our book, an entrepreneur.

That's because the essence of entrepreneurship is DOING. Entrepreneurs make things happen. In this book, we will focus on the entrepreneur who starts from scratch and the entrepreneur who takes his or her businesses to the next level.

ENTREPRENEURIAL LEADERSHIP

Entrepreneurs are people who organize and manage a business undertaking. They assume the investment and/or security risk for the sake of their dreams and hopefully their profit.

Entrepreneurs come in all shapes and sizes, yet there are some attributes that seem to be common in most of them. They are, for the most part, pretty good at getting things going. They are an excitable bunch. Caught up in the enthusiasm of their ideas and dreams, they rush forward with their embryonic plans until they actually start something. As emerging entrepreneurs they are always out there selling and telling the story of their business. Their passion drives them to reach their dream on a deadline. They certainly can organize and manage their businesses in the beginning, but then what?

Many of them get stuck. Why? Because entrepreneurs get their juices flowing from creating new things, conceiving great ideas, and putting them into action. Once the thrill is gone, so is the impetus needed to keep the enterprise going in an orderly fashion. That's why so many entrepreneurs have trouble taking their businesses to the next level. But it couldn't be more important. As you'll see, moving from entrepreneur to entrepreneurial leadership means changing your mind-set. It means becoming a leader and owning the leadership mentality that drives the venture forward, becoming the person who others want to follow, the one who keeps the energy flowing while forging ahead and trying new things. Yes, it means structure and manuals, policies and procedures, and an overall strategic plan.

It is only by getting to this point, however, that entrepreneurs can gather the fruits of their labors. Yet entrepreneurs often don't realize what structure they need to harvest that fruit because they are too busy creating and building to worry much about the details. All of a sudden, they turn around and start to see that they could easily "busy" themselves out of business. You, in fact, may be in this position right now. Not to worry; this book will show you how to truly lead, increasing enormously the chances that you'll not just survive, but thrive in the years to come.

To paraphrase President Dwight D. Eisenhower, leadership is the art of getting people to do something you want done because they want to do it. This statement is one of our all-time favorites. It crystallizes the essence of leadership. These words will guide us through this book and lie behind the entrepreneurial leadership model we are about to introduce.

As you'll see, to lead is the entrepreneur's true mission, whether that's within the marketplace, with employees, or for the society at large. Having a leadership model and course of action that has been well thought out and preplanned is the easiest way to achieve a fruitful outcome.

IF YOU'RE JUST STARTING

If your business is still but a glimmer in your eye or newly formed, read this next section carefully. We'll take a quick look at what it takes to start a business with your eyes wide open.

Research, research, and more research is the entrepreneur's version of the classic real estate line voiced so many years ago by Philadelphia's bricks and mortar tycoon, Albert M. Greenfield, when he said, "Location, location, location." Some say the most critical words in the entrepreneur's vocabulary are "stop, look, and listen." Take the time to visit, or revisit, the problem you are solving by starting a business to hear your current and/or potential customers and the marketplace. The ability to stop, look, and listen can pay huge dividends as you lead your enterprise.

The first step in any leader's journey toward success is to speak with family and friends about your idea. Remember that history's greatest leaders had advisors. Brainstorm with those closest to you; it's an important part of your preplanning process. Don't worry about anyone stealing your idea because you're only going to go to people you can trust. Besides, you know that if your concept makes sense, you're the one who's actually going to follow through and do it!

Get feedback and use it to help mold your pitch and business plan. Make sure you take notes. Set up an easel with a flip chart. Write out questions that will help you start off the session and foster communication and creativity. Ask about what trends they see, what needs people have, what products or services are off the mark, what systems of delivery should be improved, updated, or invented. You may not even want to tell them your business idea until you've drawn out some creative thoughts from the group.

By listening and watching the reactions of others about the products and services you will offer and the needs you plan to fulfill, you may be able to tweak your original idea a bit before it comes out of your mouth! Next, go out and do some more research based on what your advisors have told you. Then present your findings to people you trust. Stop, look, and listen to what they have to say and how they react. Understand that emotion always plays a large part as to why people buy, but also realize that an emotional response without proper rationale can wind up costing a lot of money.

You may want to brainstorm in order to GET a new idea for a business as well. That also takes research and should entail lots of reading—including magazines, newspapers, and Websites you would never normally read. Keep your mind open. Look at the world through different lenses. Use your capacity to innovate. Ask people what it is that frustrates them and what they'd like to make their lives easier. Think about what would make *your* life easier! Also, don't forget that today's marketplace is global. You don't have to limit your thoughts to your town, region, state, or country any longer. Entrepreneurs are just as likely to sell products and services to customers across the street as they are to businesses and individuals across the continent or on the other side of the world.

Remember, you have choices. Besides selling products or services directly to clients the "old-fashioned way" (through one-on-one relationships, sales representatives, and associations), the Internet has created the ability to set up your own global store. In your research, make sure you check into how many businesses sell internationally. Spend some time looking at the revenues being made by companies that would not exist if it were not for the World Wide Web as well as the trends and preferences in different countries and cultures.

Who knows where the next big idea will come from? Leaders create energy in themselves and others, often from the energy they receive.

Next, having an outline of how you see your entrepreneurial trip progressing is essential. Set deadlines on your calendar for each step that will help you achieve your goal. That way, you can cross off components as you approach the opening of your new enterprise. Your first step may be research, your second, brainstorming, and so forth.

Spend some of your research time looking into your potential customer base. Learn the demographics that you will be focusing your efforts toward. Think about the products or services you will be providing and how you will get them produced. Learn about buying habits. Think about your market niche and how and when you would attack it. Take some time to see what's selling now and what your competition is doing. Get to know which segments will satisfy your entrepreneurial desires (something we'll get into more in future chapters). Will you be selling high-, mid-, or lower-end goods? Will you be directing your service to small-, medium-, or large-sized businesses? Will you be targeting your business toward a specific ethnic, gender, age, or other type of group? And ... what are their buying patterns? Look at advertising in the print, electronic, and new media. Read as much as you can about what you want to do in newspapers, magazines, and on the Web. This will help you to understand the trends in the marketplace. Learn to recognize the difference between public relations pieces and straight-talk stories. All with an eye toward how your new enterprise can become a leader in the marketplace.

These are all questions an entrepreneur needs to address *before* any results are put into a business plan or pitch.

Once you've diagnosed the marketplace and spent some time brainstorming, you can start to Mind Map. Mind Mapping is a great exercise that can help you focus on your current ideas while enabling you to use your research to take you to places you may not have thought about. It's a way to brainstorm on paper. We know that you could use Mind Mapping in your initial brainstorming sessions as well, but saving it until you've done some research helps you avoid overresearching. The Mind Map gives you a clear picture of your business idea on one flip chart page and that is key. (See Appendix A for more on Mind Mapping.)

Keep in mind that a passionate leader can often persuade others to his or her way of thinking. Not a bad trait once the business is up and running, but something that should be tempered during the fact-finding, brainstorming, and preplanning stage.

Now you're beginning to whittle away the business areas that aren't appealing. You're starting to set the course that can lead you and others down the path to success. You may even have the "stuff of dreams" just waiting to be financed.

Ah yes, money. After you've sliced and diced your research, run things through the meat grinder of your mind, brainstormed with your closest advisors, and come up with the next idea that will lead to millions, it's time to think about the dough (the money kind, not the ingredient you'll need in your bakery, if that's your entrepreneurial dream).

Money may or may not be an issue. Some companies start with hard work, sweat, and a computer. Others need a small amount of seed capital. Dan started his optical company with $1,000 ($500 from each a friend and his brother). It's now an international chain. Don started a technical consulting firm for less than $50,000. Other ventures need sizable amounts of money to get off the ground. Be realistic about your monetary needs. Too many businesses fail not because it was a bad idea, but because they ran out of money. List all your potential expenses. Leave room for a slow start and bad weather (if that could be a factor). Build into your projections an inflation rate. Be as conservative as possible. Have three sales and revenue projections: slow, moderate, and good. If you think you'll take the market by storm, don't put it in your projections—it's better to have others be surprised. Start-up capital can come from all sorts of places, from your own bank accounts and credit cards (think Spike Lee) to family and friends (maybe even some of the same people you brainstormed with) to banks and venture capital firms, and from the government. Check our resources for each chapter in Appendix A.

PLANNING AHEAD

Assuming you're now ready to start the next Microsoft, FedEx, corner deli, or law practice, keep in mind that entrepreneurs have a tendency to want to do everything themselves. That makes sense because in all likelihood that's the way the business started. But as a business grows, that catch-as-catch-can style becomes unmanageable. Yet too many entrepreneurs can't let go. They become scattered, do too many things, and at times compensate by micromanaging. During that period is when a leader recognizes that it's time to have others lead. Although it may be tough to realize that someone else can do this or that task better than you, it may not be hard to understand that it's the path toward growth.

Putting together a solid plan should prepare you and your business for growth. This enables you to see the potential opportunities for yourself as well as your staff and to build a structure that will maintain itself by projecting specific needs in areas such as inventory, employees, revenues, and the like. In addition, it will enable you to put your first team in place.

How can you have a successful team if you're the only employee of your budding enterprise? Well, you should have a lawyer, accountant, perhaps even a technology consultant, that you should list as your initial group. Every plan should have spots on the organizational chart for potential hires. All you have to do is put the job titles or areas of expertise on the sheet and you'll have the makings of growth (at least from a team perspective).

As a leader, always remember that ultimately your job is to make your job obsolete. Your model should have that element built in. Leaders with insight understand that as the enterprise grows, their responsibilities shift or increase. The only way to handle the change is to have people ready to step into their old spot so they can move up to the next.

That doesn't mean losing that good old family feeling or stopping the "Let's go for a bite after work" routine. What it does mean is beginning to realize that you're in need of a controller and hiring one, putting a person in the marketing department who has actually done something like that before, and even hiring a president or COO to run the ship and its structure. Now you, the entrepreneur, can do what you do best: create, build, direct, play, and lead.

As we alluded to earlier, one of the best ways to get your business ideas organized and directed is to create a business pitch which will lead to a full-blown plan.

CREATING THE PLAN AND MAKING THE PITCH

Creating a business pitch and a business plan, whether you're thinking of starting or have started a business, is one of the most important things any entrepreneur should do before jumping headfirst into a venture. The pitch requires you to build 10 slides that capture the essence of your business. The pitch will then be integrated into your business plan. Although it's usually one of the least favorite exercises for a new businessperson, it may be the most eye-opening and beneficial. Because many endeavors are started on gut feelings alone (which may include yours), stepping back to review your enterprise or idea is a great exercise that can save you untold dollars. We recommend that you build your business pitch first, get feedback from your advisors, and then develop your business plan. One of our recommended books is *The Art of the Start* by Guy Kawaski (see Appendix B). This will guide you through the process of building your pitch.

LEADERSHIP MISTAKES OF CLASSIC ENTREPRENEURS

Before we take you through the different elements of entrepreneurial leadership, we have some questions for you.

If you are a classic entrepreneur, stand back and look at yourself, your company, or the company you envision. Yes, that may mean that you might have to stop running around like a chicken without a head. Take a second and assess what's really going on around you.

- Are you trying to do too many things yourself?
- Do you have so much work that it seems like you're never finished?
- Do you know what you want your business to look like by the end of the year, three years and five years?
- Do you have a tendency to waste time doing tasks that you shouldn't be doing?
- Can you delegate more than you do?
- Have you lost sight of your original goal?
- Are you not as organized as you could or should be?
- Would you like to grow at a more rapid pace?

If you answered "yes" to one or more of these questions, this book will help you by giving you a roadmap to fulfill your entrepreneurial dreams.

THE EFFECTIVE LEADERSHIP MODEL

Through the Effective Leadership Model, this book will walk you through a proven process that enables you to create an organization of growth and prosperity as well as the energy to sustain that forward momentum into the future.

You will notice that each step in the Effective Leadership Model guides you through a process built from the bottom up. As the levels of the Model move to the top of the pyramid, they take you closer to the top step: Success.

Chapter 1: "Understanding Who You Are," our first step, is the foundation on which everything else rests. Without knowing who you are, how can you know what you're capable of doing? Once you have established your leadership identity, you can start to move up the pyramid.

Chapter 2: Step two is about understanding "Your Ethical Framework, Motivation, and Passion." Although step one helped you understand yourself, step two helps you gain insights into how to use your new knowledge to craft a leadership identity that incorporates your ethical, motivational, and passionate attributes.

Chapter 3: In "Your Vision for Your Business," step three, we will take you through the process of succinctly establishing how and why your business vision is created and what leadership qualities it takes to communicate your business vision consistently.

Chapter 4: "Your Mission—Your Strategy," step four, is when leaders begin to narrow their focus. Laying out why you plan to do what you do and how to do it are the tenets necessary for leaders to gather the troops and explain why the roadmap exists and how the organization intends to reach its destination.

Chapter 5: Step five, "Your Action Plan and Execution," contains those all-important tactics needed to help make sure that all possible roadblocks have been examined and analyzed as much as possible. It is the step that enables the leader to mount the steed and ready the commanders (even if it's themselves) to make sure all the correct individuals are in place to execute the action plan.

Chapter 6: Step six, "Understanding Others to Create Shared Vision and Values," is the cement that makes execution possible. An effective leader understands the members of the team and places the proper persons in the correct positions within the organization for it to reach its goals and objectives. Knowing employees' strengths and weaknesses, motivators and attitudes, and interests and passions is the essential glue that creates the bond of shared vision and values for results-oriented teams.

Chapter 7: "Empowerment and Expansion of Your Employees and Your Business," step seven, is an essential part of any leader's insight into

Figure I.1
The Entrepreneur's Leadership Model

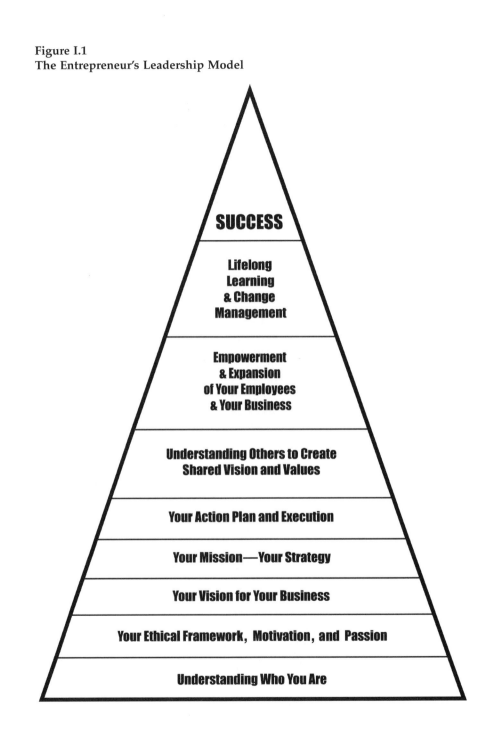

SUCCESS

Lifelong
Learning
& Change
Management

Empowerment
& Expansion
of Your Employees
& Your Business

Understanding Others to Create
Shared Vision and Values

Your Action Plan and Execution

Your Mission—Your Strategy

Your Vision for Your Business

Your Ethical Framework, Motivation, and Passion

Understanding Who You Are

how to expand the business. A leader leads; therefore, empowering others enables the leader and the business to grow through the leader's direction and appropriate delegation. By setting a tone of growth, for not only the business but also the individuals within it, the entrepreneurial leader builds strong employee trust that empowers people to create new avenues of growth, establish broader parameters of risk, and enable a state of excitement and idea generation that fosters higher employee retention, pursuit of new markets, and greater revenues.

Chapter 8: "Lifelong Learning and Change Management," step eight, addresses the need for continuous individual, entrepreneurial, and corporate growth. Because the environment in which business exists is not static, neither is the process by which we deal with the changes our enterprises encounter. Through continuous lifelong learning, we open our entrepreneurial minds to even newer ideas that will help the leader deal with change (market shifts, employee needs, and government regulations) and help the leader create the next level of stimulation and growth needed to sustain the venture.

Chapter 9: Finally, step nine: "Success," addresses what it means to succeed and how to manifest the attributes of leadership within the successful enterprise. What does the entrepreneurial leader do now that he or she has gained a measure of success? Where does one go from here? How does one establish the next level of success? Who should be the standard bearers moving forward? These are a sample of the questions we tackle at the top of our pyramid. Because reaching the peak also means that the entrepreneurial leader is now standing on the pinnacle, it also means that it's the easiest place to lose one's footing. Our last step addresses the successful aspects of the leader's achievement and the discussion of how to stay firmly on top.

As we take you through each step, you will understand how to obtain entrepreneurial leadership in a reliable and organized manner:

- Recognize what your entrepreneurial dream is.
- Identify the tasks involved in the day-to-day operation of your business.
- List the priorities necessary to fulfill those tasks.
- Envision where you would like your company to be at year's end, in three years and five years.
- Create a realistic understanding of the strengths and weaknesses of all employees, including yourself.
- Break down your typical day including time charting of your activities for each day for a week.
- Have a complete understanding, for yourself and your employees, as to why you started the company and what your values, vision, and mission are for it.
- Assess how organized, or disorganized, your enterprise, office and/or work area is.
- Build a culture of camaraderie and creativity.

- Become a leader that people enjoy and willingly follow.
- Understand other important factors that will help your entrepreneurial leadership skills move your venture into the future.

THE ENTREPRENEURIAL VOYAGE

As we guide you through our leadership model, we will offer a series of stories on businesses we founded that illustrate the difference between a managerial mind-set and an entrepreneurial leadership model. We will give you examples of how we used our leadership model and some suggestions that you should try. These stories are meant to give you practical, down-to-earth, usable skills and learning resources to help you lead, not just manage, your business enterprise. And they will show you the value of having a plan to succeed. In this book, we'll follow two personal examples to illustrate the value of planning—not to mention inspiration and hard work.

For Eyes

When Dan decided to introduce an entirely new concept for selling eyeglasses into the marketplace, he first went to his boss at the optical company where he was employed. His boss said the idea would never work. Of course, the boss was selling his products quite well for five times what Dan was proposing, so why should he want to try it? Dan even went to some friends who had the same reaction. But when speaking with others the response was very different. As he researched the eyewear field, checked demographics, revenues, population trends, and other pertinent information, he felt his idea became more and more viable. There were other factors propelling him as well, which we will discuss in later chapters. Another aspect that helped was having a timeline. These were all elements in Dan's preplanning process that ultimately led to success.

Learning Resources

In the mid-1980s, General Motors Corporation (GM) was converting its automobile assembly plants to higher technology in an attempt to eliminate quality problems that had become apparent when competing against the Japanese auto industry. At the Wilmington, Delaware, assembly plant, managers began the conversion in early 1985. One of the human resource problems was training the skilled trades to run and maintain the new robotics, to learn new computer languages, and to address safety issues related to the new technologies. When implemented, the Wilmington Assembly Plant would become the most technologically advanced automobile assembly plant in the western hemisphere. However, GM was experiencing problems in plants where they had made the transition to robotics, and they were looking for a comprehensive training solution that would ensure the skilled trades could run and maintain all this expensive, high-technology equipment. This situation presented Don with an opportunity and a challenge that he readily accepted. Throughout the book we will provide examples from this project as well to illustrate various points.

With the information in this and the other chapters of *The Entrepreneur's Guide to Successful Leadership* you can begin to structure yourself and your company for long-term success.

You'll also learn quite a bit about yourself. You may be great at one phase of the business, but as the entity expands, not so wonderful at the tasks needed in the new environment that growth brings. Leaders know that and adapt. We'll give you the tools you need to make important decisions about filling key slots, as well as everything else that contributes to a humming business.

Let's begin.

1

Understanding Who You Are

As entrepreneurs, we have a certain excitement in our being. We recognize that our ideas can become reality with a little hard work, persistence, and the support and help of those around us. That entrepreneurial excitement is a wonderful feeling, and it's one that we must explore as we continue to lead our business or start a new one. Let's look at the first step in our Leadership Model, Understanding Who You Are.

Hard work and perseverance come from an understanding of what gets your juices flowing, how you behave, and what it is you do best. Entrepreneurs have the same goal of becoming a success, but what that means to each of them and what route each takes to achieve success can vary greatly. To understand ourselves first, is an essential stepping-stone to effective leadership.

As entrepreneurs, we are always looking for the next business opportunity or how to grow the current business. Sometimes that opportunity comes from surprising places. Years ago, Don had successfully led and managed a technical training project for General Motors. After four years, he decided to return to his entrepreneurial roots. Steve, one of Don's partners, showed him an ad from a Philadelphia newspaper for a business to buy. Don was surprised; the business was a landscape maintenance company in suburban Philadelphia, and it had been twenty years since Don had shut down one of his early ventures, a landscaping company. Upon reflection, however, Don realized the passion was still there; he was sold on the idea of getting back into his old field of endeavor. Steve had understood Don's continued interest in landscaping despite the years of working for General Motors.

When For Eyes, Dan's optical company, started to increase its customer base, revenues, and geographic reach, he understood himself and realized that it would be better if he didn't work the production machinery in the laboratory. He enjoyed making the finished product, but it was more beneficial to everyone concerned if Dan, as the head of the company, focused on his strengths: building the image of the organization, training retail managers, working on the company manual, formulating district and regional

Figure 1.1
The Leadership Model—Understanding Who You Are

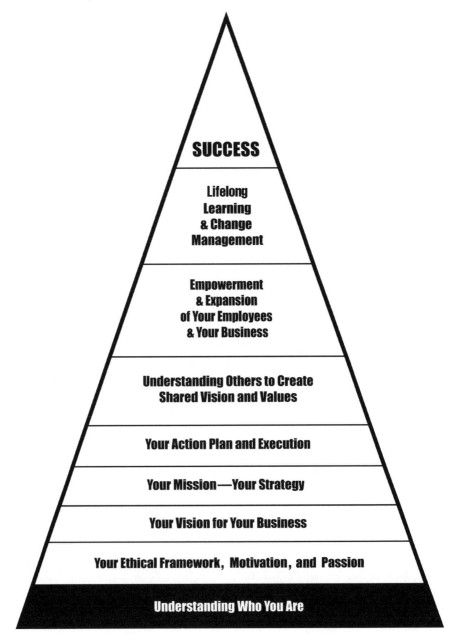

manager responsibilities, and spending time outlining and fulfilling his marketing and public relations strategies.

To continue growth, Dan had to make sure that he brought on board someone who enjoyed and had the aptitude to learn the technical side of the business.

THE ENTREPRENEURIAL INVENTORY

> You cannot teach a man anything, you can only help him to find it within himself.
>
> —Galileo

The initial step to understanding yourself is to take an entrepreneurial inventory of yourself. The first item in that assessment is honesty. Once you've become dedicated to being up-front with yourself, you're on your way to personal and business growth. Here are some questions you should answer first:

- Do you have self-discipline?
- Do you like to make decisions?
- Do you like people?
- Do you enjoy competition?
- Are you a leader who plans ahead?
- Are you an outgoing person?
- Do others say you are the kind of person who gets along with other people?

The answers to the questions above set the stage for an inventory. Your attitudes, values, interests, and motivators about life and business have a major impact on how you see the world and your role in it.

Do you get excited about learning, finding out how products work and services help people, and reading books about facts, figures, and other elements that enhance your knowledge? Are you driven to ensure you make a proper return on your investment of time, money, and resources you've expended on yourself and your business? Or do you care less about processes and more about building a better mousetrap?

Perhaps your penchant is to help people. Your energies are directed to making sure that society is a better place, and your enterprise, without regard to profits, helps those in need by creating products and services that are affordable to those who must have them. Maybe you're into the beauty of life and its surroundings including everything from physical space to personal attire and even to the harmony of the environment. You may be an individual who enjoys power, position, social status, directing yourself and others, and bringing order to business and life.

Last, you may thrive on following processes, rules, or strict instructions including such things as manuals, religious text, or proven approaches and techniques.

Think about what moves you into action. Think about what you are passionate about. Think about your skills and knowledge and your interests. What is it that makes you want to succeed? Of the attributes we've discussed, one or two of them will become your primary motivators. That doesn't mean that the others aren't part of your being; it only means that your top two (sometimes three) are the attributes that truly drive your entrepreneurial energy.

WHY YOU DO WHAT YOU DO (SELF-MOTIVATION)

While you're looking at what motivates you, think also about why. Usually your parents, surroundings, and cultural background play a major part in why you do what you do. If your mom or dad was an entrepreneur, your tendency may be to follow in their footsteps. However, if your parents worked in the nonprofit sector, you may find that the reason you want to start an alternative school may come from your parents' social leanings. Our friend Kate started a preschool for underprivileged children, in the same manner as her mother founded an adult day-care center for older people in need.

Of course, there can be exceptions. Every apple doesn't fall close to the tree. There are always some that roll down the hill and find a whole new land where other apples fear to tread.

Once you've figured out what gets your adrenalin rushing, you'll recognize what got you into your entrepreneurial world and what will or will not keep your juices flowing. If, however, you find that you are trying to talk yourself into a venture that others are convinced will work, but makes you feel uncomfortable, think again. If something is outside of your value system, it would be a recipe for disaster. Even if the venture succeeds, you may open yourself up to everything from general anxiety to serious health problems along the way. Consider your instincts carefully before you travel along an entrepreneurial path.

Motivation must come from within, and it must power you forward. Search your memory and study those times when you felt happy. We all want to be happy and need to find positive feelings toward ourselves and our employees as much as possible. The opposite is also true: We need to avoid the negative feelings of being down. A leader looks to the positive and sends clear messages to everyone that we are on the right path. You get energy by painting a positive picture of the future.

Matching your passions with your entrepreneurial skills sets the stage for business success. If you're the one making the decisions, stick with what will make you most comfortable, happy, and contented.

HOW YOU DO WHAT YOU DO (COMMUNICATION)

The path to understanding who you are as an entrepreneur includes not only why you do what you do, but also how you do what you do. This second element is also about perception. How you perceive yourself and how others perceive you can make the difference between the success and failure of your endeavors. Once you understand that, playing the "role" of an entrepreneur takes on a broader meaning.

Hopefully, you have begun to see what motivates you in a clearer light. Now, let's move over to the perception element. Most people perceive themselves differently from how others perceive them. In some cases, the difference may be small, and, in other cases, it may be surprisingly large. In either situation, you should try to make the gap between your self-perception and the perception of others as small as possible.

Your behavior is the basis by which others decide whether or not to interact with you (or at least want to interact with you). The expression "you can get more with honey than with vinegar" is an easy way to understand and remember what your behavior, as an entrepreneur, can bring. (Of course, one person's honey is another person's poison, and we'll discuss that as well.)

People tend to play roles. Recall Shakespeare's quote: "All the world's a stage; And all the men and women merely players; They have their exits and their entrances; And one man in his time plays many parts." It gives us an interesting overview of life. Within the acts and scenes of our lives, we perform many different parts within the play. The entrepreneur is a role we play, and, while we're in that role, our actions may differ substantially from that of father, mother, husband, wife, brother, sister, son, daughter, teacher, student, etc.

The way you act as an entrepreneur affects everyone who works with you, including prospects, clients, employees, vendors, and other stakeholders. Your actions really do speak louder than words. Those actions make people want to work with you, purchase your products and services, sell to you, promote you, interview you, and increase your chances of success.

Your behavior will portray who you are differently to different people. Part of the disparity is your perception of them and part is their perception of you. Your entrepreneurial behavior can fall within four main categories: domineering, effusive, consistent, or detailer. Within these four categories, there's really no good, bad, better, worse, right, or wrong way to behave.

Each category's intensity can vary from low to high; however, only one category will be your core behavior whereas the other three add to your behavioral texture.

Domineering

You may be someone who is oriented to results and task completion—and domineering, impatient, or curt in your conversations as a result. You may be a person who instills fear in others, someone who gets angry while forging ahead—sometimes without coming up for a breath of fresh air.

If this is your behavior, you should remember that those who work with you, sell to you, or buy from you may be put off by the way you act. They may be intimidated enough not to come to you with suggestions on how to make your business grow, fix problems that you may be having as your enterprise goes through its paces, or not want to work with you because of the anxiety you create. Understanding that your actions can negatively affect your organization is a good reason to look at yourself realistically and to adjust accordingly.

This is not to say that being domineering is a bad way to behave. Actually, domineering people quite often plow through adversity to reach their goals. They pull up their boots and get on with the tasks at hand, bringing others along with them. A highly domineering person may get angry and explode at themselves, an employee, or a partner, but they're also usually quick to forgive and move on.

Effusive

Some entrepreneurs are extremely outgoing and display an effusive behavior. These "effusives" are people oriented, emotional, love to have fun, experience new things, and are folks who enjoy talking about themselves and their businesses.

A person who manifests a high degree of this behavior tends to need to be liked by others and is, therefore, a bit more trusting than most. This trait can create problems if those you trust don't fulfill their obligations to you and your entrepreneurial venture. To make matters more complicated, the "effusive" may have trouble reprimanding others or giving direct feedback because of their need to be liked. An effusive entrepreneur could wind up paying the price of wanting to be liked by having others run all over him or her. If you tend toward this attribute, be aware that your emotions may decrease your efficiency.

However, the "effusives" also skew toward being exceptional salespeople, especially if they also have a high degree of "domineering" in them. The combination of wanting to complete tasks along with being a good conversationalist helps entrepreneurs sell their products and services to a sizable section of the market.

Consistent

There are many entrepreneurs who have consistent behavior. These folks are the "steady-as-she-goes" entrepreneurs. They are people oriented yet introverted, organized, and possessive.

Because they are "people people," they also tend to be trusting like their effusive counterparts and indirect in their feedback as well. However, very little tends to rattle their cages. These are entrepreneurs who will plod along through the storm until they've reached their objective. They don't lead the charge in an extroverted way like the domineering businessperson but reach the same place by checking the signposts and walking within the maze. The "domineering" may have cut down the maze on their way to the goal while the "consistent" keeps it intact.

The "consistent" will be on top of what needs to be done and when to do it. They will also remind everyone of their schedules, tasks, and the deadline of the project at hand.

Detailer

Our fourth entrepreneur is the "detailer." These people have all the facts and figures. No comma will go unnoticed, no screw un-inventoried, no action uncalculated.

They are of the scientific mind, setting their entrepreneurial thoughts toward the task at hand in a methodical manner. Their directness, critical analysis, zest for procedures, information, and formulaic approach create products and services that tend to be extremely precise. The rub is that they also have a tendency to miss deadlines because of the desire for perfection. Although "very good" may be acceptable to their clients or customers, the "detailer" entrepreneur may be very uncomfortable putting out anything that isn't exact.

These folks make excellent products and give wonderful service. However, they must be aware of the realistic marketplace, deadlines, and how their exacting and critical behavior affects those around them.

As we see, entrepreneurs come in many value systems and behaviors. The trick for the budding entrepreneur is to know his or her own behavior and attitudes along with the knowledge of how others behave and what motivates them and to use that information to grow their organizations. How does one do that? The answer is by becoming an entrepreneurial chameleon and subjugating their own behaviors and attitudes while going into someone else's world to relate to the person from their perspective. Because we know that people buy from people they like, the idea is to become a reflection of your prospect, client, employee, customer, or whomever you need to work with to make your venture successful. Relating to people from their perspectives and behaviors makes it easier for them to buy into whatever it is you may be building, growing, or selling. The entrepreneur who masters that art will certainly have an easier time getting employees and customers, and generating revenues and profits.

Understanding who you are and using that skill to further your goals enables you to be in better control of the leadership process and of your successful entrepreneurship.

LISTEN!

In the mid-1990s, Don had an opportunity to contract again with General Motors. The keys to making the second project successful were his understanding of himself first and listening to his client second. This may sound easy, but it was not. As with many business opportunities, Don did not initially have a clear understanding of the client's problem and, therefore, the solution. He chose to take a small contract that would bring him on-site to the Wilmington, Delaware, assembly plant and give him the opportunity to listen. He opted to invest time and resources and perhaps win a much larger contract.

Listening is the most important part of communication and is a skill a leader must develop and practice every day. To really hear what was being said and what was not being said, Don had to listen intently and watch his General Motors clients. He knew that the success of the project would determine if the plant would stay open. The stakes were high, and he realized that he had an ethical obligation to help after he gained the necessary knowledge. Next, he had to convince plant management and the United Auto Workers Union management that a joint solution could work.

While on-site, he listened to everyone and got their ideas about the new Saturn project in Wilmington and the team concept that had to be implemented. This required Don to listen to the workforce's concerns and fears about changing the roles of labor and management after a fifty-year history. That was the challenge because the track record of installing a team concept at other automobile manufacturing facilities was not good.

The solution required months of time and careful thought. Don combined an understanding of himself and his company and an understanding of his client's new vision to create a workable solution. He devised a customized four-day team building program along with a personal coaching program for management.

SEVEN ELEMENTS

To execute successful leadership you need a strong understanding of yourself. The Seven Elements of Successful Leadership™ (The Seven Elements), below, developed by Dan to help his clients with leadership issues,

Figure 1.2
The Seven Elements of Successful Leadership™

is a way of doing that. Integrating The Seven Elements into your day-to-day interactions with employees, vendors, and customers will maximize your effectiveness and help ensure the success of your enterprise. We will illustrate examples of The Seven Elements throughout each chapter of this book as they are integrated into all nine levels of our leadership model.

1. Communication
2. Controlling Growth
3. Setting Goals/Solving Problems
4. Time/Schedule Management
5. Team Building
6. Delegation
7. Motivation

Your Ethical Framework, Motivation, and Passion

With new insights into who you are, you're now able to take a serious look at your passions, motivations, and the ethical framework that shape your life and your business. In this section, you will begin to sculpt the leadership skills necessary to build the enterprise you desire and will determine if you are really ready for the adventure called "entrepreneurship." Your actions and feelings will shape each day as an entrepreneurial leader. Flora Whittemore put it this way, "The doors we open and close each day decide the lives we live."

ETHICAL FRAMEWORKS

When we discuss ethics and morals, we're talking about those items that are inherent in our makeup. We realize that each of us has a different view of ethics and morals and, just as one person's ceiling is another person's floor, one person's unethical behavior may fit perfectly into another person's ethical framework. But there are some common denominators in just about everyone's value system: being treated fairly, honestly, and with respect.

Be forewarned though, money does strange things to entrepreneurs. Be ready for the ethical challenges. Over the years, we have experienced the old saying, "You never know someone until money is involved in your dealings."

Back in the 1960s and 1970s, ethics surged forward as a focal point for society and business. During those turbulent years, the one major motivator for many budding entrepreneurs was how their start-up ventures would fit into the ethics of that time. Today, entrepreneurs run into ethical questions and problems continually. Our world is getting "smaller" and "flatter," and our actions affect people across the globe. Many business owners wonder about the ethical consequences of their endeavors and the effect they have on our planet and on other people.

We have started companies that reflected our ethical upbringing. Dan's For Eyes optical company was based on the "people before profit" motive.

Figure 2.1
Leadership Model—Your Ethical Framework, Motivation, and Passion

SUCCESS

Lifelong
Learning
& Change
Management

Empowerment
& Expansion
of Your Employees
& Your Business

Understanding Others to Create
Shared Vision and Values

Your Action Plan and Execution

Your Mission—Your Strategy

Your Vision for Your Business

Your Ethical Framework, Motivation, and Passion

Understanding Who You Are

It was very important to him that his clients were given the highest-quality products at the lowest possible prices, that employees had fun, and that everyone involved was treated fairly. Don's landscaping corporation, Preferred Home and Lawn, was founded to serve customers and also to help employees get a college education. Preferred Home and Lawn became one of the first "environmental" companies in suburban Philadelphia. These strategies are part of our ethical makeup, which is passed down to us from our parents, friends, and society. Going against your ethical foundation can cause severe angst and even health problems.

Think of your enterprise as a reflection of who you are. If you are a person who promotes a healthy lifestyle outside of business, could you sell cigarettes? Would you feel comfortable having a restaurant that featured only high-fat, high-calorie items? It may be difficult for you to visualize yourself in either of those roles, but, if the profits were significant, would you do it?

Don faced that issue when wasteful aerial spraying of trees in the landscape business became prevalent. An advisor said to Don, "The best move now is to do tree injections instead of spraying." He stopped spraying almost immediately! He found it friendlier to the environment to feed and treat the trees directly rather than from the air. Even though it cost more money initially, that decision contributed to his company's sales growth and became a core value of all its employees.

THE ETHICAL INVENTORY

To quote Julius Caesar by way of Shakespeare: "The fault is not in our stars, dear Brutus, but in ourselves." We think Caesar got it right. As an effective leader, you need to answer the questions below to help you assess your ethical inventory:

- Will your new business undermine or support your ethical foundation?
- Will your ethical framework motivate you in your new business?
- Do you strive to share your ethical framework with others as part of your business mission?
- Can you communicate your ethical framework to all your stakeholders?
- Will you leave a legacy that you will be proud of?

Ethics has become such a hot point in our society that Congress has actually had to legislate it. The Sarbanes–Oxley Act was in response to the mess created by the Enrons of the world. It is sad that we, as a society, had become so ethically deprived that we had to pass laws to force businesses to act in the best interests of their stakeholders.

Your employees will observe and imitate your ethics and morals. Be aware of how you conduct yourself as an effective leader; your actions will be evaluated by those who must follow them. You must model the behaviors you want to see from your employees, so be consistent. When you model the behavior you want, it becomes a habit for you and your employees.

The ethical leader creates an atmosphere of trust and a feeling of comfort for those within the organization. That kind of atmosphere encourages growth and creativity. When Don started a business that would become a four-year project for GM, his brother-in-law showed him a Macintosh computer. He remarked, "It looks like a breadbox," and laughed. Then, he looked under the hood and realized that his whole team needed to see it. By trusting his brother-in-law's opinion, as well as the thoughts of the rest of his team, the company moved to desk-top publishing to help GM.

The ethical leader creates a positive energy field that will attract others to follow. Unethical behavior actually can create health hazards for those affected by the acts, including employees, their families (we all know that angst rolls downhill), customers, vendors, and other stakeholders. It's common to hear of employees leaving a company (or customers refusing to buy from a company) because of the owner's unscrupulous ways. A negative energy source will drain the life out of a company. Putting ethical conduct as an example of your business's credo is a great way to set a tone of positive leadership for everyone involved with your company.

Your ethical framework should include things such as honesty, empathy, keeping your word, and respect.

Honesty

The old saying "Honesty is the best policy" is true, especially in business. Cheating, lying, and stealing, whether done maliciously or not, will always get you in the end. Once word gets out that a business owner has been dishonest or unscrupulous, it becomes very difficult to attract new vendors, clients, employees and other stakeholders.

Make sure that all documents are clear and concise without too much jargon, which can confuse others and create misrepresentation and the image of an unethical company. Advertising and promotions should reflect exactly what your company will sell or service. Actions that can be interpreted as bait-and-switch tactics will drive customers away quickly from your door.

Know all the regulations, laws, and rules for your industry, or hire the right professionals to help you abide by all the statutes that are pertinent to your business. Being dishonest may, on some occasions, not be the owner's fault, but ignorance of the law is no excuse. Lee Iacocca said, "I have found that being honest is the best technique I can use. Right up front, tell people what you're trying to accomplish and what you're willing to sacrifice to accomplish it."

Empathy

Empathy is called a good bedside manner in the medical profession. We would sooner go to a doctor who shows us empathy than one who doesn't, even in those cases where the nonempathetic doctor may be more qualified. Atticus Finch, in *To Kill a Mockingbird*, stated: "If you just learn a single trick, Scout, you'll get along a little better with all kinds of folks. You never really understand a person until you consider things from his (or her) point of view—until you climb inside of his (or her) skin and walk around in it."

Put yourself in the shoes of your customers, employees, suppliers, and other stakeholders. People like to deal with folks who they feel will understand their plight, situation, or need. Empathy will resolve problems, create goodwill, and instill confidence in you and your company.

Keeping Your Word

Nothing is more frustrating to those you deal with—including yourself—than people who can't be depended upon to do what they say they will do. Keeping one's word builds trust. "My word is my bond" is a common phrase that may be taken lightly in some circles, but, in business, it can be the difference between success and failure.

Keeping your word also means having the ability to say "no." Because some folks have behaviors that are based upon the need to be liked (as we saw in the previous chapter), their tendency is to say "yes" to far too many requests. Often that leads to an overloaded schedule and a situation where nothing seems to get completed. Saying "no" is another way of keeping your word. It tells the other person that you respect them enough to be truthful and admit that you will not be able to help them at that particular time. As Henry David Thoreau said, "Be true to your work, your word, and your friend."

Respect

Have you ever gone into a store and been treated by the staff or owner in a disrespectful manner? Does it feel demeaning, unethical, and unnecessary? Showing a lack of respect toward your customers, employees, and suppliers is the quickest way to begin the demise of your business. Whereas honesty, empathy, and keeping your word may take your stakeholders time to figure out, respect reveals itself immediately. When you show disrespect, the reaction on the part of those you depend upon for the growth of your business can be equally as fast. It doesn't take long for a customer, employee, or supplier to turn around and leave.

Respect starts by respecting yourself. Author Ayn Rand said it this way, "If one doesn't respect oneself, one can have neither love nor respect for others."

PARTNERSHIPS

One area of conflict that may arise is the conflict of the ethics, motivations, and passions between partners. Before starting any partnership or corporation containing more than one founder, make sure that all parties involved have a clear and concise understanding of each person's motivations, ethics, and passions. If those topics are not openly discussed and dissected, then fledgling organizations can run into problems from the very beginning.

Find out if your ethics are in alignment. Play out scenarios containing situations that may create ethical dilemmas. Very few, if any, businesses do this at the beginning. If they would, some of them may not start, or they could avoid future problems. Openly discuss why you want to start your new endeavor and what you would like to get out of it. Lay your ethical, motivational, and passion cards on the table. Otherwise, they may come back to haunt the enterprise later.

As your company grows, it is critical to have these ethical conversations on a regular basis. Don's Learning Resources (Learning Resources Technical Training Consultants Inc.) grew at over 20% per year, and the two principals (Steve and Don) agreed to meet twice a year (rather than the usual once a year) to write down and agree to the key business strategies. These sessions were intense, causing many long nights, but Steve and Don always ended with complete and mutual understanding. They believe these sessions contributed greatly to their success and friendship.

ETHICAL LEADERSHIP

The Golden Rule is "Do unto others as you would have others do unto you." Leaders know how to motivate, delegate, and show others the way. Most of all, they create an atmosphere of stability, honesty, dependability, trust, respect, empathy, and accountability. They know what the future holds and create an atmosphere of fun. An ethical leader treats people fairly, thinks about the impact his or her actions will have on others, and gets people to perform tasks that need to be completed because the people doing the tasks want to do them. Leaders with high ethical standards know that, besides leading their team, they are also part of it. Once your customers, vendors, and employees see your leadership tendencies, abilities, and the positive impact you have on others, they will almost always willingly follow. Ethical leaders create reputations for themselves and their companies that foster loyalty on the part of all stakeholders. And loyalty helps to build customer bases, employee morale, expansion, and revenue.

PASSION

Passion is that uninhibited love and desire for whatever it is that you want to do. It's the fuel of your dreams and the energy that causes you to keep going. Passion is behind every great entrepreneurial leader and their ventures. Passion can be your desire to learn, build, discover, create, experience, grow, make money, lead, write, perform, or any other factor that causes you to see things before they happen and then make them happen. Ben Franklin's desire to discover and learn helped him harness electricity, Bill Gates' passion for computers and what they could do has helped him become one of the wealthiest men in the world, and Stevie Wonder's passion for writing and performing has given us the gift of his music and made him a very successful businessperson. The list is endless.

Understanding your passion is one of the most important factors toward your success as an entrepreneur and a business leader. It can lead you to many places. The trick is to make sure it leads you in the right direction. Passion without realism can cause great difficulties for you as well as those who are affected by your dream. The need to recognize that some of your passions may lead to entrepreneurial deadends will help you ferret out the businesses that can create disastrous consequences.

Dan once had a client who had a passion for health spas. She loved everything about them and visited them on a regular basis. Her love for spas was so overwhelming that she soon wanted to have one of her own. She didn't do much primary research such as speaking one-on-one with potential clients, other spa owners, suppliers, spa-specialist travel agents, real estate brokers and agents, or other folks who could have given her solid advice. She neglected doing any substantial secondary research to find out important things like demographics, psychographics, spas in her region, spa associations, suppliers, menus, and other information that could help her make an informed decision. She went ahead and became the proud owner of her own day-spa. Within a year she was in trouble.

She came to Dan in a panic and asked how to turn her business around. It was obvious to Dan upon her arrival that her passion had overridden her rational decision-making processes. She had opened her spa in a resort community in New Jersey. Her customer base was small, her marketing negligible, and her business plan and profits were almost nonexistent.

With lots of research and some repositioning, within six months the business was booming. However, Dan discovered that her passion was for the spa culture, but not for running a profitable spa herself. Her comment to him was, "We can't handle all this business, too many people are calling!" Not in a joyful—how great it is that we're busy—type of way, but in a panicked, angry manner. Her true passion became apparent when she had the opportunity for an interview on a widely viewed television talk show targeted precisely to her female demographic, but chose instead to head off to France to visit, you guessed it, a spa!

Your desire to be an entrepreneur can be driven by passion but must come along with an understanding of the business world and the hard work that will accompany your endeavor. A dream derived from passion fueled by fantasy cannot be made into a profitable business.

HAVE FUN

Having fun can also add to that productivity. Fun in business makes it easier to be motivated to work. It enables everyone to own the passion and live the dream. Fun, laughter, and enjoyment are some of the primary factors in employee retention, in many cases even more than money. It's difficult to feel the passion and gather the energy of motivation when work is drudgery. Most entrepreneurs who later become leaders in their field will tell you how much fun starting their business was. Sure, it was hard work and time-consuming, but most also will agree that, if it weren't fun, it wasn't going to happen. It's not unusual to hear entrepreneurs relate stories about leaving their prior employment because "it just wasn't fun anymore."

Be aware of the "funability" of your endeavor. Ask yourself if you'd want to work there if it weren't your business. Spend some time with other entrepreneurs and ask them how they create a fun atmosphere at their companies. Boring is not in the passion or motivation dictionaries. Having an inviting and fun environment helps you, your employees, and your customers have that desire to return day after day. Fun is the best form of communication.

At Don's landscaping business, he had pool parties and barbeques every two weeks during the landscaping season on Wednesday afternoons. They were a family affair with spouses and children as well as employees. They always ended with a great game of volleyball and a lot of laughs. The fun environment carried over into teamwork at work.

There were some financial gains to the fun, however. To get a full day's work done by 2:30 PM, everyone had to hustle. As a result, Don discovered how to change some processes so that they became more efficient. He improved quality and productivity—because everyone had fun.

"Funability" does not mean all games and laughter. Work must get completed, tasks accomplished, and revenues generated. However, all these items are easier to fulfill when there is a lightness that permeates the business. Lightness can be as motivating as any other aspect of an enterprise. A feeling of tenseness and anxiety can be counterproductive and cause higher turnover rates.

Mary owns an information technology consulting firm in suburban Philadelphia. Although she and her employees work diligently to service their clients and complete projects, meet deadlines, and create proposals, she also makes it a point to have a party every Friday starting an hour before the normal close of the workday. It's also a normal occurrence to have stacks of chocolates in the middle of the conference table for sales, brainstorming, and production meetings. Mary has had wine experts come in from California for wine-tasting seminars complete with the appropriate foods. Her holiday parties are always a treat, and, because she's in a little town that's known for its restaurants, she quite often takes her employees to lunch or dinner. Not surprisingly, her employee turnover rate is extremely low, the company's productivity is high, her employees voluntarily work more hours than they have to, which, consequently, enables her to pay them quite well!

Relating your passion and motivation to those you work with (whether your employees or vendors) through lightness and fun can go a long way toward helping you build the business of your dreams. When you exude those attributes, people want to be around you, buy from you, sell to you, and experience your energy.

KEY POINTS AND LESSONS LEARNED

☑   Write down your ethical framework.

☑   Share your ethical framework with your partners and other stakeholders at the beginning of the venture or project.

☑   Model the behaviors you want to see from your employees.

☑   Honesty really is the best business policy.

☑   Walk in your customer's shoes to build a strong mutual bond.

☑   Keep your word. Keeping your word builds trust, and trust is more valuable than gold.

☑   Respect yourself, your employees, and your customers.

☑   Lead with passion and fun to gain loyalty from employees and customers.

3

Your Vision for Your Business

What do you visualize for your business? As you enter the world of the entrepreneur or grow within that world, what is the vision you see for the concept you call your business endeavor? That vision must paint a clear picture of the future business you seek to create. What do you see for the business in a year, and, more important, three years down the road? Your vision must paint a picture that is compelling. Jack Welch, former CEO of General Electric, once said: "Good business leaders create a vision, articulate the vision, passionately own the vision, and relentlessly drive it to completion."

Your vision for the business is a forecast of how you see your enterprise emerging out of your imagination. You must be able to see it in your mind's eye. It must be visceral, too. You need to picture yourself there and hear it, smell it, see it, feel it, and almost taste it. Vision must capture your passion and motivate you to make it happen. Your vision is your "dream on a deadline," and it compels you to action. What results do you see for your enterprise at least three years in the future when you develop your vision statement?

We have all heard of, or seen, great visionaries, who predict the future, understand trends and preferences, recognize niches and exploit them, and have a knack for feeling the reaction of people before things happen. And your vision must make an emotional connection to the "marketplace." Friends, those attributes are what the vision for your business should be about!

Stand back and look at your idea, whether it's in full swing or a budding thought, and think about what you see the future holding for you and it. Again, you should look out at least three years. Your vision will drive your mission and enable you to explain the basis for your business to those who will join you as employees, investors, customers, landlords, and other stakeholders. There's no better way to enlist others into your fold than to have a clear and concise vision for your business.

Don's vision for his landscaping company truly compelled action. Preferred Home and Lawn changed many of the "rules" its competitors lived by and helped it grow over 20% per year. When Don started the company,

Figure 3.1
Leadership Model—Your Vision for Your Business

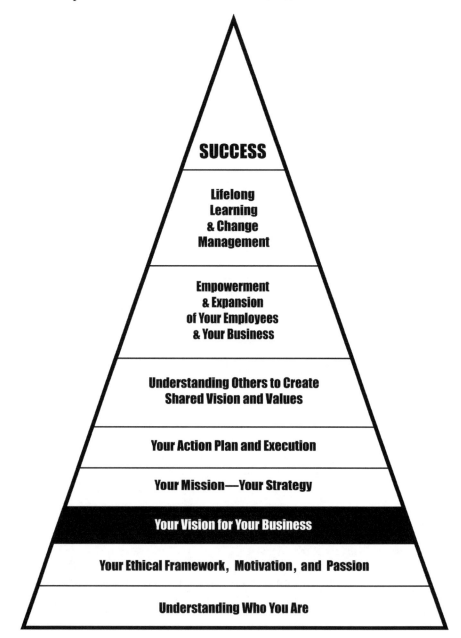

it had no market identity. Its vision of an environmentally friendly company owned by the employees and based on a team concept became its identity. The perception of the firm as an innovative, environmentally concerned landscaping company took hold. And that vision allowed it to expand its service capabilities and moved it to catch hold of the latest trends in landscaping. People buy based on emotion, and Don and his people made sure the marketplace knew their story.

A muddled vision will lead to a muddled enterprise. A clear vision allows you to steer the car in the proper direction, but a muddled vision will let you wander all over the road and sometimes drive on the wrong side. In other words, your vision is the yardstick you must use to measure success, not your mission. What will the business look like in three years? How will it be different from now? What do you have to achieve in three years to consider yourself a success? We have often run into companies whose employees complain that management has no idea what they're doing, mainly because the actions of top executives have strayed so far from the vision upon which the organization was founded as to create confusion moving forward. Perhaps you've been involved in one of those enterprises and felt the frustration firsthand. If so, realize that, to avoid problems for your business in the future, it's up to you to create a clear path in the present.

The term "vision statement" has been beaten to death by entrepreneurs and organizations; however, it can help direct you and your company in ways that build loyalty, growth, and consistency if it is handled correctly. We want to share with you a process of building a vision statement that has worked for us.

It is common for entrepreneurs to put together their vision without knowing its impact on themselves and other individuals who may become, or are now, part of their organization. We have seen individual entrepreneurs or entrepreneurial partners formulate their vision statements without the input of employees, leading to irrelevant and confusing ideas. These statements are usually filled with self-aggrandizing adjectives and bland objectives, which are then framed and hung on the wall for all employees, prospects, and clients to see as they enter the organization's office. We want you to have a living, breathing vision that all of your stakeholders buy into. If it were easy to do, we would see more successful businesses. So roll up your sleeves and get ready to do some heavy lifting.

VISION QUESTIONS

To avoid stereotypical vision statements, you should spend some time understanding your goals, client base, and expansion plans. Remember why you founded your organization and what you planned to do in the future for your employees, the community, the company, and yourself.

Ask certain questions of yourself and, if applicable, your partners, your advisors, your employees, and your other stakeholders:

- What effect will my vision have upon me, and the people who work within my organization?
- How often will I and the employees refer to it?
- Is it relevant to the folks who read it?
- Was it established for the benefit of clients, stakeholders, employees, all three groups, or just me?
- Whose input went into the formation of the vision?
- Will it hold up over time?
- Does it reflect the values, beliefs, ethics, motivation, and passion of the organization as well as my own?

Don will walk you through the actual process he used to build the vision for his Learning Resources company. Then, we will show you the process was used to develop a vision statement in a client's company. These examples will give you insights and guidance on constructing a vision statement for your company that focuses your efforts and gives you the energy to get you going every day.

LEARNING RESOURCES COMPANY VISION STATEMENT

Now, Don will look at his Learning Resources company and the steps he took to build the vision statement: First, my partner and I established the ground rules for our employees and all of our subcontractors who worked with us on the L-Car project at General Motors. As the leaders, it was important that my partners and I valued every team member's participation and contribution. Listening carefully to each other was a key to crafting a vision that everyone would buy into. The process had to be non-judgmental, and everyone was encouraged to express their ideas and opinions about the General Motors L-Car project at the Wilmington, Delaware, facility.

Working on-site at a General Motors assembly plant in a union environment, our goal, as Learning Resources company, was to create a learning environment that would help the plant move from a moderately productive traditional environment to a highly productive, high-technology facility. When our four-year project was over, the GM plant in Wilmington was one of the most technologically advanced plants in the world. More important, they were producing world-class, profitable cars. We made a firm commitment that, once everyone got a clear understanding of the vision statement, we would reference it every day in everything we did. We emphasize that the vision that we created for Learning Resources company before the project started directly led to the project's total success after four years on-site at the General Motors Wilmington, Delaware, Assembly Plant. We could not have accomplished this feat without listening carefully to all the members of our team and building a powerful vision for our business together.

We began the process by getting our ten-person team together, first at a local Chinese restaurant and then with follow-up meetings at the Learning Center on-site at the GM plant. We also had individual meetings with each team member at my home or theirs to learn their personal opinions and desires. These off-site meetings were the key to building a vision that everyone was committed too. We took the time to build the vision over several months and got the buy-in of all participants, and the vision statement lasted for the entire four years on-site. Even though our mission and tasks changed every six months as the project grew, it was the vision that drove the enterprise to succeed. We were driven to understand all the dimensions of the problem that General Motors was trying to solve. At the local level we needed to understand the learning problems faced by the hundreds of skilled-trades workers at the assembly plant.

The next step was to put out a first draft of our vision that expressed our understanding of how we would help transform the Wilmington Assembly Plant to high technology. Next, we wanted everyone to express what they understood our company to be doing in the plant and what the plant's future in three or four years would look like. Once we had captured this information, we began to clarify the vision through a series of informal and formal meetings. We made sure to include into our vision our values and the ethical framework of the business.

We discussed our principles and values and how they related to our task of implementing an adult learning model for the General Motors union workers. Most of the skilled-trades workers had not been in school for thirty years, and, in fact, they told us they became tradesmen because they didn't like school. We needed to create an adult learning center, not an "educational" training center. Don remembers a conversation with Jim, one of the GM trainers: "Don, why are there carpets in the center?" Don's response: "Because, we want it to be like home." This was part of our vision—create a learning environment and treat everyone with professionalism and tender loving care.

At the time, this approach was controversial in part because we were using computer-managed instruction, which was brand new. But use of leading-edge technology was integral to our vision. We needed to create self-paced, individualized instruction that allowed the learner to proceed through the learning process as fast as he or she could. We spent many hours discussing our role and how it aligned with our client's strategic objectives. One of the keys to our success was having the skilled tradesmen's first experience with computers come at our learning center under the caring eyes of our team of adult learning specialists.

Next, we wanted to get each employee's and subcontractor's perspective on two questions. First, why did they work for Learning Resources? Second, why did they want to continue to work for Learning Resources on-site at General Motors? These two questions must be asked when you are building a vision statement for your business. It gets to the heart of the matter. Why am I here and why do I want to stay here? As a leader, you must take time to listen and shape the vision statement around the team that will get you to a successful conclusion.

Our intention for the vision statement of Learning Resources was, first of all, for our employees and subcontractors. Second, it was for our client, General Motors, and our other stakeholders. We must emphasize this point because the vision statement that we created allowed us to grow and to be a valuable asset to General Motors and to the hundreds of skilled-trades workers that came through the Learning Center.

Once we had completed the development of the vision and had a clear understanding of it, we spent money on our employees and subcontractors to provide them with the best training available to help us run our project. Throughout the process, we kept the General Motors Technical Training Manager involved in how we were developing our vision statement. His understanding of our vision created the flexibility we needed as the mission of the technical training effort grew and changed. Suddenly, we were involved in plant safety—a new mission. We were ready. This subject was not in our mission originally, but our vision allowed us to say, "Yes, we'll help you with safety." Early in the project, one of our associates arrived at the plant with an Apple Macintosh computer and showed the Technical Training Manager we could build job aids for the robots. Within six months, we had a dozen GM technical trainers working with our staff to build job performance aids. Eventually, we would share job aids with other GM plants using the GMF robots. This development was directly related to the vision: getting management and labor involved in the process of using technology as a tool to improve plant maintenance.

Now, let's turn our attention to a client of ours and the process we used to help them build a vision statement.

PROCESS TO CREATE A VISION STATEMENT

Dan recently spent three days with the employees of an expanding entrepreneurial company. All the executives, including the founder, were in attendance in addition to most of the people who worked there. The purpose of the conference was to enable everyone to contribute to the company's vision statement.

He started by laying out ground rules:

- Everyone's input was needed.
- The entire process would be nonjudgmental.
- Attendees could say, in fact were encouraged to say, exactly what was on their mind without retribution.
- The statement would be decided upon by the end of the conference and implemented.
- Open communications would continue after the conference.

Dan began the process by defining the vision statement as an understanding of how the participants saw the present and future of the company. He wanted them to look into the future, but not, in today's quickly changing business climate, more than three years.

Dan discussed a list of the company's principles and values with the owners. The list included why the company was started and what was behind its growth (internally and externally). Together, they dissected each word or phrase for relevance to the company, the industry, and the people in the room. Dan asked questions such as:

- Did these principles and values move people to buy into the company's industry view?
- Were they the reasons why the individuals worked for the company?
- Did they symbolize discomforting ideas for the folks in attendance?

He asked everyone to look at these questions from the perspective of the employee:

- Why did they work for the company?
- Why did they want to continue to work for the company?

It doesn't matter if you have employees or not, someday you may and it always helps to view your vision from the perspective of others, including potential employees. Your vision should inspire all your stakeholders, and most important, your employees. Ralph Lauren put it this way: "A leader has the vision and conviction that a dream can be achieved. He inspires the power and energy to get it done."

The common conception is that vision statements are made for clients and prospects. In fact, they are secondary to your thoughts and your employees' buy-in. Vision statements are first and foremost the fuel that drives the company from the inside out. If your vision statement has all the bells and whistles for customers and prospects but has no relevance for yourself or your employees, you may as well hang it facing the wall.

Dan spent time assessing the beliefs and values of each attendee and how they fit into his or her view of the company. He then analyzed the past strengths and weaknesses of the company. After extensive discussion, he moved on to evaluating the organization's current strengths and weaknesses, including the most important aspects of the company as seen by the participants.

After listing the insights involving current strengths and weaknesses, Dan defined where the attendees wanted to see the organization go from its current position. By breaking into smaller groups, they were able to begin forming their own vision statements by listing each group's principles and values as vital components of the greater vision of the company.

He reviewed and prioritized each group's principles and values and identified common elements.

From all the information collected, Dan carefully crafted the company's vision statement. He took everyone's suggestions into consideration, and the final outcome made for a successful meeting where all the participants understood and helped to create the vision.

However, we must caution you about a postconference problem that can destroy all the goodwill generated by a successful meeting. Entrepreneurial leaders must be aware of the "drop-the-ball" syndrome.

Time and time again, entrepreneurs and their organizations follow effective conferences with—nothing!

People go back to their old ways and habits. The effects of the new vision statement wither away like the motivational seminar that has no follow-up. Attendees stay pumped up for three days and then begin the deflation process.

It is imperative to keep the lines of communications open. There must be a process to check in with attendees to make sure they understand that their suggestions, thoughts, and views are valued.

In the case of Dan's conference, everyone received his or her copy of the organization's vision statement quickly. They were thanked for their input and reminded that they were integral in writing it. In addition, a program of intercompany communication was installed to make sure that the vital interaction that created the document continued.

The final outcome was not only a statement, which was relevant for the founders, clients, prospects, and employees alike, but also a group of people who felt an ownership in the vision of their company.

Whether you have one employee or one thousand, the process of understanding your entrepreneurial vision is the same. It's all about breaking down your values, ethics, motivations, passions, interests, and attitudes into a concrete knowledge of where you see yourself and your enterprise in the future. How you see your company getting there will be left to your mission, strategy, action plan, and other elements.

Earlier in this book, Dan spoke about his optical company and the credo, "people before profits." That was and is a part of his, and our, value system, but it was also a part of his vision. It enabled him to visualize a vivid picture of giving people a place where affordable eyewear would be available. His entrepreneurial leadership would spark a personal and business movement to help others. Dan's clear vision (please pardon the optical pun) was the impetus that drove him to create the company. He constantly kept it in the forefront of his thoughts as he worked toward the day when we would be open for business. Harvard professor Rosabeth Moss Kanter put it this way: "Vision is not just a picture of what could be: it is an appeal to our better selves, a call to become more."

EMBROIDERY COMPANY VISION

A close friend of ours named Sharon wanted to start an embroidery company. She would constantly speak about her love of embroidery, the art behind it, her passion to be in the business, and her desire to do something she loved.

The first thing we wanted to know was whether she had taken the time to understand the hours involved in starting an entrepreneurial venture and if she was ready to put forth the effort and leadership skills to make it a reality. She assured us that she had and was. Before delving into action plans, the market, competition, and the like, we knew that Sharon's vision for her business was a foundation that had to be put in place first.

What was the mental picture that Sharon had created from her imagination that would move her forward? We needed to know what she saw. We needed to know the vision of the future she sought to create.

We started by asking her if she could put into words how her business would reflect her passion, motivation, values, beliefs, and ethics. Her answer was: "My business would reflect a culture of honesty, creativity, fun, making money, and growth." She added that all those factors were important elements in her life and that, for many years, she had envisioned that embroidery, which had been and still remained a hobby, could become her career and that she could incorporate all those aspects into her venture.

We then asked Sharon if she would start her new business as the only employee. She told us that she would, but that her neighbor and best friend Karen would be willing to join her (if and when revenues made it possible, because Karen was a single parent with two children and a full-time job). Of course we had to know if Karen shared the same ideals. Her answer was that the two of them had spent many days going over the aspects of business that were most important to both of them and that their conclusions were the same: honesty, creativity, fun, making money, and growth (personally and professionally).

We also wanted to know how Sharon's husband and four children felt about her entrepreneurial ideas. She mentioned that they were all for it.

Our next step for Sharon was homework. We asked her if she would sit with her family and run the vision she saw for her business by the entire group and give us their input. We suggested that she also ask her family that if they were employees how would they think her vision would be relevant to them?

Many entrepreneurs don't take the time to recognize that their families, regardless if they are spouses, children, siblings, or parents, are stakeholders. Anyone who is affected by the business has a stake in it. That stake can be monetary, but it can also be emotional. We started our leadership model by asking you to focus on *"Who you are."* And this is why it is critical that you have your family's support and understanding.

The following week we had our next meeting with Sharon and her comments were quite revealing. She told us that her family (as relatives and potential employees) saw the vision a bit differently than she had. Yes, they agreed that honesty, creativity, fun, making money, and growth were important, but so was fairness, relaxation, camaraderie, hard work, and the ability to expand as an enterprise (which, they explained, was somewhat different from the way they interpreted the term growth that she had originally presented).

She stated how gratifying it was to get her family's thoughts and how she never realized the importance they played as stakeholders.

After a few weeks of boiling down all the components, we derived a very clear vision of how Sharon imagined her soon-to-be-started venture. "Our company vision weaves creativity, fun, fairness, friendship, and growth, into the fabric of opportunity and a profitable experience for all of our stakeholders."

Those words were the guiding light that propelled Sharon to start her business. She posted it on her computer, refrigerator, and a few other prominent places in her home and home office. She also gave a copy to Karen to remind her of what was in store for the future. Its relevance has held up over time, and its ability to help people visualize what Sharon's vision is has remained clear.

Your vision statement is more than a statement about your vision: It's a statement about you and your goals. What do you want out of your life and how can your entrepreneurial ideas help you reach your objectives?

When you think about your life and how you want to lead it, it's a good idea to understand that creating the future you desire is all about how focused you are. In addition, you must recognize that the ultimate accountability rests with you, and how you will lead yourself and others to achieve the outcome of your dreams.

Be realistic about your vision. Striving to get to the moon when all you have is a wagon won't cut it. But if the goal for your business is to sell your own designed and handmade mugs on the Internet and to be known as the "King of Handmade Mugs," well, that sounds like a reasonable venture, providing, of course, that you have access to a potter's wheel, kiln, and packing.

DYNAMIC VISION

Your vision and vision statement are living items, which means they can change with market conditions and other causes that you may not have expected. Just to be clear: Your vision is a mental picture; your vision statement is written.

When Dan started the optical company, his vision was simple: "People before profit—The highest quality eyewear at the most righteous prices anywhere." As the market took notice, however, and the company started to grow, he and his team had some choices to make. Do we stay small and try to keep the client base at a constant level, or do we take advantage of the exposure and positioning and expand the vision?

Dan and his leadership team chose the second. The vision entailed keeping their original values, passions, motivations, and interests, and also adding new insights such as the vision of becoming a national company with other vertically integrated subsidiaries. They visualized new delivery techniques along with a culture that espoused a continuing feeling of family for all their stakeholders.

As the business grew, so did the vision. There's nothing wrong with revising your vision. Sometimes, it can save you from disastrous results.

Take a moment to think about how books were sold to the public in the 1980s. If you were in the retail book business, your vision may have been to have stores where people could relax, read, purchase the items that appealed to them, and have a pleasant experience while doing it. Your vision would also probably include making a profit and employing people who enjoyed the world of books.

Today that vision would be expanded quite a bit. As we all know, the world of relaxation in most local bookstores includes a café where people can read books, magazines, and other periodicals while drinking their favorite coffee, tea, or other drink and snacking on some treats or eating a complete meal. Many books in the stores are not only of the paper variety but can be purchased on CDs. Now, that means a separate department for CDs which in many stores also translates into a music department. Most bookstores also have Websites where you can purchase the books online without having to step into a brick-and-mortar location. Plus, many books aren't made of paper or audio CDs at all; they are e-books that are read on your computer screen, which also can be bought online.

This example shows us that the bookstore of the past has, in many cases, been transformed into a broader concept, a concept that took a change of vision. Somewhere, someone said, "You know what I visualize? I see a store where people can eat, drink, read, and buy books and music while having a good time. They can bring their kids, and we can have a section for the little ones with toys and small chairs and tables, they'll have their own environment. Plus, if they can't come in, how 'bout if we use the Internet to sell them stuff?"

Can you imagine what that initial vision was like? Can you see the vision statement that must have accompanied those thoughts?

We must realize that what happened to bookstores was indeed a change of vision and that it wasn't an entirely new situation, just an expansion on an existing one.

Being able to enhance your vision helps you get out of ruts, enables new thoughts, and makes entrepreneurs do what entrepreneurs do best, create and lead business in different and exciting directions.

PRODUCT OF IMAGINATION

Inventions are born out of vision, some of our most imaginative items, things that changed our world, were brought to us by people who had the vision to think differently and lead the way.

Look around you and think about how things have always been done in the business you are currently involved with or are thinking of starting. Run the process through your mind, perhaps taking the time to write down your observations. Now, think about how those same items could be done more effectively and efficiently. Broaden your horizons, think differently, play, enjoy, become a kid again. How would you approach the situation if you didn't know how it was done today?

Vision is imagination, being able to look into the future. As we said earlier, being realistic is important, but just as important is being imaginative. Don came to a Small Business Development Center (SBDC) in 2000 with the responsibility of creating a new vision for its training program. Imagination drove him and the leadership to challenge and forge a new, powerful vision. They saw themselves in the future helping thousands and tens of thousands of entrepreneurs, not hundreds. They saw themselves becoming the leaders in creating learning opportunities over the Web. And, they envisioned an e-blended learning model supported with partnerships with local SCORE chapters in the region. The staff would be certified by the Kauffman Foundation to use its excellent entrepreneurial materials. This model would be based on adult learning theory, not an educational model used by most SBDCs. In 2007, Don's SBDC was recognized as a national leader by the Small Business Administration in Washington.

Take time to brainstorm. Sit with friends and family and throw around ideas. A Mind Map is an illustration of words and phrases connected to a central idea. Imagine a bicycle wheel with the hub being the main idea and the spokes, as well as branches coming off those spokes, adding other creative thoughts to the core concept. Using Mind Maps to figure out new and exciting ways to build upon your original thought, can lead you to places you never realized were there. (See Appendix A for more on Mind Mapping.)

In an entrepreneurial class at a university in Philadelphia, Pennsylvania, Dan uses Mind Mapping. He will put a business idea on the blackboard that was suggested by one of the students. First he asks about the values, motivations, ethics, and passion behind the business. Once all the students understand the reason the would-be entrepreneur wanted to start the enterprise, he then asks for ideas that would help to expand the concept while staying within the focused area. Within a half an hour, the original idea will have grown into quite a venture. Each new branch of the Mind Map takes the class into new and exciting arenas which are complimentary to the main business.

Dan advises each and every student to be aware of the core values that caused the first idea to sprout, to keep that vision on the "front burner," but not to forget how the other suggestions were derived. They grew out of the same values, motivations, ethics, and passions as the original business.

The exercise that follows is usually revealing. He has the class create the vision statement for the business. Although many students want to include all the branches of the Mind Map within the vision statement, ultimately it is the core business that the focus of the statement revolves around. The class also realizes that, when the main business contains the vision, any other ventures that are derived from it would undoubtedly have the same ideals incorporated within them. When all the elements contained in a vision statement become evident, it is difficult to lose the basic ethical, moral, and motivational tenets that the business was founded upon.

GLOBALIZATION

The Internet has made commerce international, and the information we need instantaneous. Any entrepreneur's vision is only limited by his or her imagination. Selling internationally should be considered a part of any new or growing businessperson's market as long as the products or services are transferable to different cultures, ethics, morals, and values.

It is common for us to be asked to advise businesspeople about international commerce only to recognize that their business model, products, and/or services would not fit within the culture of their targeted market. Being aware of the transferability of your vision is as important as the vision itself when it comes to dealing globally.

If your vision includes doing business throughout the world, take the time to investigate the cultural underpinnings of the regions, countries, and groups whose markets you would like to penetrate. It's imperative to remember that what you may think is perfectly fine could create problems in other cultures.

Dan once had a client, John, whose vision and vision statement included helping the world by taking a certain food product and introducing it to other countries. John and his team believed that the nutritional value and taste were excellent. Transporting the product was simple enough, as was storage. However, what they failed to realize was that their enthusiasm had blinded their vision about one major factor. No one in their target market had any desire to buy their product because it was outside of their cultural practices. Cultural preferences can change, but limiting your market to one that is culturally closed to your product or service can create extreme hardships for your business and derail the best-intended vision statement.

To succeed, they had to redirect their vision to something more realistic. Up went the Mind Maps, out came the brainstorming sessions, and within a few weeks John and his team had a new and realistic vision to rally around. The vision enabled them to do the planning, research, and other necessary elements to focus their efforts on a new vital position.

Relatively soon, John and his team's new vision was bearing fruit. They were selling their products to a willing customer base in areas they hadn't thought about prior to reworking their original vision statement. In fact, within a year, they had entrenched themselves so well in their new markets that their products were gaining quite a bit of attention and starting to get noticed.

Taking a broad view of the vision upon which you base your enterprise is a great way to avoid problems. Look at the entrepreneurial road that you intend to travel, or are currently on, and survey the landscape. Your vision is like a compass; it will help to guide you through the wilderness of business. It's meant to keep you on the correct path. It is a living thing and, just like your compass, it can set you on the right road. Sometimes, it enables you to see an adventurous trail that entices you. At those times, you may follow the new trail that calls you while your compass continues to inform you of your general direction. Vision-based entrepreneurial leadership is what we have focused on in this chapter. Business leaders who fail to create a compelling vision for their business, which integrates their employees' ideas and values, will not succeed in today's business climate. Our next chapter will focus on mission and strategy.

KEY POINTS AND LESSONS LEARNED

- ☑ Your business vision is what your business will look like in the future. It is the compelling reason for your actions and the support of your stakeholders.
- ☑ Involve your stakeholders in writing your "vision statement."
- ☑ Review your vision statement regularly (annually at least).
- ☑ Your family is a key stakeholder even if they don't work for the company.
- ☑ Vision is a moving picture, not a still photograph. It must accommodate change and retain its relevance.
- ☑ Your vision is only limited by your imagination.
- ☑ Your vision is the compass of your business.

Your Mission—Your Strategy

Well, you've done it—you've taken the time to understand who you really are. You've also analyzed your personal ethics, motivations, and passions. You've even looked into the future and solidified your entrepreneurial vision. Now what?

THE RULES OF THE GAME

It's time for the games to begin! It's time to get down to the nuts and bolts of what it takes to set your leadership ship sailing onto the entrepreneurial sea of business. That's right, business is a game, and you need to know the rules.

Your mission and strategy are the steps that begin to turn your vision into reality. We know that entrepreneurs tend to be creative folks. We can come up with an idea every fifteen minutes (if not sooner) and set our minds into translating those thoughts into a vision of the next multimillion-dollar enterprise faster than you can say, "Sam Walton started with one store and look at his idea now." We do it all the time. Visualizing success is what makes entrepreneurs such a fascinating lot. But people who can take those visions and turn them into the next Starbucks, or at least the neighborhood beauty salon whose schedule is starting to fill up fast, are a special breed.

Mission is the thing that says, "Here are the tasks you need to do to start cookin'." In other words, "I've seen the future. This is the direction I want to take to get there." The strategy is the thing that tells us how you are going to accomplish your mission and move you towards achieving your vision. Former eBay CEO Meg Whitman put it this way, "A business leader has to keep their [sic] organization focused on the mission. That sounds easy, but it can be tremendously challenging in today's competitive and ever changing business environment. A leader also has to motivate potential partners to join."

THE MISSION STATEMENT

Suppose it's the aforementioned beauty salon that you'd like to start. You've seen it a thousand times in your mind. You can visualize yourself

Figure 4.1
Leadership Model—Your Mission—Your Strategy

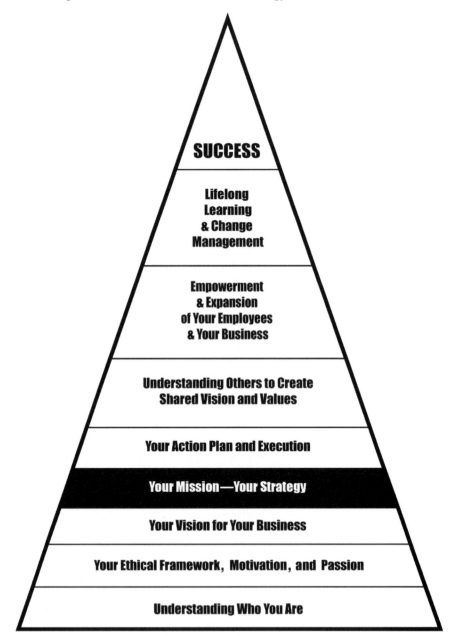

SUCCESS

Lifelong
Learning
& Change
Management

Empowerment
& Expansion
of Your Employees
& Your Business

Understanding Others to Create
Shared Vision and Values

Your Action Plan and Execution

Your Mission—Your Strategy

Your Vision for Your Business

Your Ethical Framework, Motivation, and Passion

Understanding Who You Are

greeting people, cutting their hair, coloring, shampooing, making your customers your friends, enjoying work, getting paid for your efforts, hiring folks who "get it," the whole nine yards. You can see the colors on the wall and hear the sounds of the salon working. To get there you have to figure out what your mission really is, and what your three key strategies are.

If you look at your vision from afar, you'll realize that you'll need a road map to get you there. That map will have the items that you need to follow to help you arrive at your destination. This is achieving your dream on a deadline.

Another way to look at it is to think of your mission as the mortar that holds the bricks of your vision together. Strategy is a tool, like the carpenter's level or the plumb bob used to build a plumb and square house.

DRAFT THE MISSION

Let's pretend we're your partners, and our job is to come up with the first draft of the company's mission. The first thing we'd do is look at our Vision Statement: "To create the most innovative men's and women's hair salon in the region." For those of you who are wondering, our vision doesn't mention anything about customer volume or profits because we're using the "people before profits" approach that Dan used with his optical company. We figure that, if we do all the right things, we'll be busy and making money. Next, we brainstorm (again) to come up with the items that can help propel our vision into the enterprise that we've dreamed about.

Here we go: How will we attain our vision of becoming the most innovative salon?

1. By learning the latest techniques in hairstyling through classes, seminars, and other forms of continuing education.
2. By reading the latest fashion and hairstyling magazines.
3. By using only the finest products and latest methods.
4. By hiring only the most qualified individuals who meet our standards and reflect our philosophies.
5. By caring for our customers in ways that endear us to them, including salon hours that make it easy for them to be our customers, and asking for their thoughts, ideas, and feedback on services we provide or that they would like us to provide.
6. By working with our vendors to learn about new products and to sustain relationships that create an environment of mutual respect.
7. By being in the forefront of style, quality, fun, ethics, and standards so we can be proactive in our approaches to our customers and their families, our employees, the media, the community, and other stakeholders.

As you can see, that's a pretty extensive list of ideas, but it reflects some very concrete building blocks that can help our idea get off the ground with some traction, as long as we have a solid strategy behind it.

All seven of the points listed can be called our Mission Statement. If, however, we'd like to boil it down to a few lines, we could craft it by taking key features and stating them succinctly.

The mission statement cannot be written in a vacuum. We must consider the outside world and the reality of the current business climate as we build this mission statement for the salon. So, we got outside feedback as we worked with our team at the same time. Now we are ready to mesh everyone's ideas a bit further and come up with:

Our Mission:

Through ongoing education, exceptional employees, outstanding customer care, superb vendor relationships, an atmosphere of fun, and the finest products, we will proactively use our expertise to enhance the style and energy of all of our stakeholders to be recognized as the region's most innovative hairstyling salon.

There you have it, five lines that sum up our seven points as they relate to our vision. It tells us what we intend to do to make our dream a reality. The one thing it doesn't do is inform us as to the strategies we'll use to achieve it. Keep in mind as you build your mission statement that all successful entrepreneurs are problem solvers and create unique solutions to business problems. Lee Iacocca directs us to think about this when it comes to a mission, "We are continually faced with great opportunities brilliantly disguised as insoluble problems." There is often great opportunity for entrepreneurs in problems that appear to have no solution.

Our mission is an overview that exists under our vision. Remember Sharon's embroidery company's vision from the previous chapter:

Our company vision weaves creativity, fun, fairness, friendship, and growth into the fabric of opportunity and a profitable experience for all of our stakeholders.

As we said in Chapter 3: "Your vision statement is more than a statement about your vision; it's a statement about you and your goals. What do you want out of your life, and how can your entrepreneurial ideas help you reach your objectives?"

Earlier in this chapter, we discussed how your mission statement expounds on your vision by showing you what tasks you'll need to perform to arrive at your statement's ideal. Look at the difference between Sharon's vision statement and our salon's mission statement. Can you see how Sharon laid out her dream and how we've written what we need to do to fulfill our salon's mission?

With your mission under your vision, you have begun to set the foundation for actualizing your new venture.

A number of years back, Dan helped form an oil and gas company. The enterprise was a joint venture between Dan's private group and a foreign government. Sitting around a conference table, representatives from both parties discussed the vision of the organization. Here's what the final outcome looked like:

> To create an oil and gas joint venture that will benefit both partnership groups as well as the people who will be affected by their decisions.

That vision is about as straightforward as one can get, yet it embodies quite a bit. To form an oil and gas company is not an easy venture. It's also not easy to make sure that those affected by its creation benefit from it.

The mission quite clearly stated what the tasks would be in order to drive the enterprise forward.

> We are committed to building a company that will create a cleaner environment for all inhabitants throughout the region. Through the wise and careful utilization of our resources, new technologies and facilities, we will work diligently to clean the air and water, create well-paying careers for our employees, help the area spawn new and related businesses, and build new and better schools while generating a fair profit for all our shareholders.

This mission statement gave us a clear overview of how we wanted to do things and in what direction we wanted to go. By investing in the region's oil and gas resources, the company's intention was to clean up the mess left by previous organizations. Pollution in the area was terrible, people needed jobs that would become careers, the region's schools were in need of upgrades, and we were aware also that, once the oil venture took hold, we had an obligation to help form ancillary businesses to service the workers and their families.

Whether you're starting an oil and gas company, a salon, an embroidery firm, a day-care center, or a supermarket chain, what you do with your vision and mission statements can spell the difference between success and failure.

STRATEGY

One of the most important ways to ensure a successful leadership position for you and success for your company is to have a solid strategy in place. Planning your strategy and implementing some initial steps will help you understand your market and assess the way you'll penetrate it. It will give you insight as to what it will take to staff your enterprise and what resources you'll need (monetarily, physically, and emotionally). And the investigation will result in an approximate timeline to get it all done. Strategy is a critical component of all business success, and the implementation of strategy allows you to build your enterprise.

This strategic overview will help you set the groundwork for our next chapter's subjects: Your Action Plan and Execution.

Many people think that planning out a strategy and devising an action plan is the same thing. Not so. You have to know how you're going to set up your actions before you actually put them in place. Think of it from a military perspective: Would you lead your troops into action without having a strategy first? And, once you do lead them into action, you would most certainly want to have a plan to execute those actions.

Here's a metaphor that is popular today: "dancing with your partner to beautiful music in front of a large audience." When we talk about vision, mission, and strategy, think of that metaphor. Each concept works independent of the other, yet they work together in a complex system of moves and countermoves, driven to the music and the rules of the dance. To be successful, each concept implements and extends the next in sequence to execute the dance. It's interesting how leaders plan to lead while others plan to be led. Entrepreneurial leadership takes planning to enable creativity and growth to flourish.

CREATE STRATEGIES

"A sly rabbit will have three openings to its den" notes a Chinese proverb. When you think of business strategies, think of a simple, small number, like three. Every business needs three strategies that will help it succeed with the mission in the short term and drive to the ultimate success of the vision. More than three is too many. We humans can juggle two or three balls; more than that and they start to fall. We easily can keep three things in our memory bank and work on them every day. In this chapter, we will show the relationship between vision and mission and why strategy is critical to your success.

Don used three strategies to achieve success at the Small Business Development Center (SBDC). All SBDCs have the mission of reaching out to help entrepreneurs start and grow their enterprises. They accomplish this mission by providing one-on-one consulting and educational events. When Don arrived at Kutztown University SBDC, he decided to treat this as an entrepreneurial endeavor.

The center faced a large demand for its services but had scarce resources. The classic problem Don and his team at the center faced: How do we reach more entrepreneurs with fewer and fewer resources? How do we provide help that genuinely has a positive impact on the business? How do we provide this in a timely manner?

The three strategies used, in order of importance, were (1) E-blended Learning (technology), (2) a strategic partnership with three SCORE Chapters (resources), and (3) using curriculum materials from the Kauffman Foundation (educational component). Don combined the three strategies into one driving force that enabled the creation of learning opportunities.

The result of these strategies was to make Kutztown SBDC a recognized national leader among the thousand SBDCs (www.kutztownsbdc.org). The Website went from 50 visits a week to over 2000 in four years.

Dan created a strategy for expanding For Eyes after recognizing some success factors in Philadelphia. It evolved by realizing that his core client base was university students and those individuals of college age who then spread the word to their parents. The parents in turn told their friends and colleagues.

As Dan expanded into new areas, he targeted his initial marketing toward university communities. His secondary marketing efforts were then focused on the surrounding communities, including the business and suburban areas.

This enabled him to quickly expand across the United States and overseas.

STRATEGIC ELEMENTS

The need for strategy can take you by surprise. A number of years after selling his optical company, people began asking Dan to help them build their companies. At first, it was purely a one-on-one, "Sure I'll help you," advisory type of thing, but soon he realized that this was a situation that he'd have to address by creating a formal business. (In fact, many of you may be faced with the same situation. You start with an avocation and, before you know it, you have the potential for your next business.)

After figuring out the vision and putting the mission in place, it was time to get the strategy together. As you'll see, strategy is more than an operational plan—strategy is involved in the very start-up of a business. Here are the first two steps Dan took.

Create a Name

Create a name for the business (which you may or may not have done before you devised your vision and mission—you'd be surprised how many people do not pick a name until they're just about ready to open their enterprise). Your name could reflect a number of things:

Define what you intend to do. (Think of Waste Management, For Eyes Optical, America Online, Whole Foods Market, etc.)

State who you are. (Think lawyers, consultants, doctors, etc.) This also works if you have a well-known name or intend to create your brand around you. (Examples are Trump and the many enterprises that bear his name, Campbell's Soup, Bloomberg Radio, Macy's, etc.)

Become remembered not for what you do or who you are but rather for the uniqueness of the word or words. (Think of Google, Häagen-Dazs, Tazo, and Zippo.)

Enable customers to know something about you by creating a contraction or combining of words. (Examples are Duracell, Comcast, Facebook, and Softsoap)

State the power, energy, or other attribute of the product or service you wish to sell. (Acme Markets, Zenith, Crest, and Hallmark come to mind.)

Use the initials of your enterprise. This option may work better once you establish what those letters actually stand for. (Examples are International Business Machines is now known as IBM, the National Football League is known as the NFL, General Motors is frequently called GM, and PNC, a banking institution, stands for something few people know: Pittsburgh National Corporation.)

Dan chose Professional Management and Marketing Corporation for the consulting organization he started. It said what the company did. However, after adding two partners, Dan thought that maybe it would be a good idea to change to the names of the three partners. Before they went through all the work required to do it, they, like any good marketing firm, first researched to see what clients, prospects, and the general public thought about the rebranding. Their findings confirmed that the new name created a greater impact, so they changed it. It should be noted that they didn't actually change the name of the corporation itself. Instead, they filed a "Doing Business As" (DBA) or "Trading As" document with the state, which allowed them to open a bank account, accept payments, create contracts, and sign documents using the new name.

Lay Out a Budget

Projecting your first three years is a valuable and revealing exercise—and it's an exercise in strategy. Sit down and lay out how much revenue the organization is projected to take in and how much money will be needed in the first years of business. Being realistic is extremely important. Spend a substantial amount of time analyzing your capabilities to handle the business you forecast. Estimate the behavior of your competitors and the competitive environment. Forecast the need for your product, your company's differentiating attributes, and how much office space you'll need (even if you're working at home).

Determine what types of office equipment and supplies you should have, what it will cost for utilities, how much money should be used for travel and entertaining prospects and clients, and the amount you may have to spend on marketing (advertising and public relations). Consider who you'll be hiring, from professional advisors to employees, and if additional employees are in your plans. To put it in accounting terms: what do you project your fixed and variable costs to be? Have you used a bottom-up approach to forecast your sales? Will you need a bank loan or investors' capital to start or grow your business? As we mentioned, lay out your projections into three sets: slow, moderate, and good.

Without a memorable name to make positioning your business easier in the minds of consumers and a realistic budget, it becomes extremely difficult to succeed in a competitive marketplace. Once the name and budget strategy components are defined, it makes sense to look at the concept and the process of building a list of strategic partners and putting together a "Success Team."

STRATEGIC PARTNERS

As you develop your three key strategies and write your strategic intent statement on an index card, you may need to find strategic partners.

Every business owner has potential strategic partners that can obtain mutual benefits from partnering together. Don's landscaping company, for example, partnered with an Agricultural Extension Agent of Penn State University. This was part of the strategic intent and one of the core values about using the best outside resources to assist in becoming an environmental landscape business.

You should make a list of potential strategic partners followed by mutual benefits of a partnership and, most important, a plan to start to build those relationships. Some of these will develop in months and some may take years. Dan had one case where he partnered with someone after 14 years of knowing each other.

THE SUCCESS TEAM

The Success Team is made up of the professionals who will surround you and help you implement your vision, mission, and strategy. Having a Success Team is essential in today's business environment—and it's also an element of strategy because your advisors can help you succeed faster and more grandly. Our Mind Map of the key members of the Success Team can be found in Figure 4.2.

Accountant

Search for and hire a good accountant to help figure out what type of entity should be created. The accountant can help you establish whether the

Figure 4.2
The Entrepreneur's Success Team

enterprise should be a C-Corporation, an S-Corporation, a Limited Liability Company (LLC), a partnership, a sole proprietorship, or some other type of entity. Each one of these entities has different tax implications and selection of each is an especially important decision for legal, accounting, medical, or other professional companies. Your accountant also can work with you to review the reality of your projections, set up tax ID numbers, and advise you on what types of taxes you'll have to pay.

We have had many accountants during our business careers, and the best of them had the following characteristics:

- They were Certified Public Accountants (CPAs) that worked with small businesses similar to ours.
- They were up-to-date with the latest thinking on taxes.
- They were willing to be members of our success team.
- They were willing to work with our attorneys.

Your accountant should be willing to help "educate" you to the world of finance and accounting. We strongly suggest that you interview at least three accountants before selecting the one that is "right for you." We located our accountants through referrals from other businesspeople and through the local Chamber of Commerce.

Attorney

Search for and hire a good attorney to set up the new entity and give insights into other items that may be legally required, such as filing the entity's name to get a trademark or registration mark, applying for a patent (if applicable), and having agreements between partners or shareholders in case of dissolution of the entity sometime in the future. Dealing with the often-sticky issue of dissolution is always better to do at the beginning before emotions enter into the picture. A lawyer can explain the legal process for doing business in other states and countries (something accountants would be involved with as well).

Artist and Graphic Designer

Search for and hire a good graphic artist to design your logo, business cards, letterhead, envelopes, and Website. Be sure to take a look at their work (their portfolio) and get an understanding of how they work. You want to know that your logo reflects what you have in mind for your business. Insist that the artist spend time with you to get a complete understanding of what you and your business entails. From those sessions your logo and tag line will emerge. Many times the artist will design what they believe your business is about or what they want your business to reflect rather than what it actually does. Ensuring a logo and tag line that matches your business is one of the most important things you do for your business!

As we all know, perception really is reality. Companies will pay a king's ransom for a logo that sets them apart from their competition, firmly plants them in the minds of their current and potential customers, and enables them to portray a leadership position in the marketplace (perhaps even before they actually attain that position). The business cards you give out, the letterhead you send, the look of your Website all portray who and what your organization is about.

One of our favorite graphic designers says that the marketing materials you hand out act as a security blanket. The materials give you the confidence to pitch your business to bankers, potential partners, and customers.

Some graphic artists are also proficient in Web design, but not all. It may wind up that the graphic artist with whom you decide to work may not be the most capable Web designer. That means that you'll have to choose another team member who can handle that task. That person will be your Webmaster.

Webmaster

Your Webmaster is one of the most important members of your Success Team. Depending upon your business, the World Wide Web can be one of the most cost-effective vehicles to market, communicate, and manage your enterprise. For the consulting business, we reviewed three potential vendors and their work and asked for references.

You will need to build a relationship with your Webmaster and get him or her to speak in a language that you can understand (which is not always easy with technology-driven folk). Moreover, the selection of a Webmaster may also need to be based on his or her ability to program and create databases that will help you manage your growing business.

Your Website is your window to the world and creates in the user's mind a perception of your business. As we said earlier, perception is reality. It is critical that you make an emotional connection with your customers. With your Website, this emotional connection can be achieved with pictures or utilizing streaming video. Your Webmaster can also build online forums, or online newsletters. Both of these are a cost-effective way to reach your current and potential customers. It's important that your Webmaster listen to what you are saying, understand your vision and mission, and is open to addressing your changing needs.

Banker

Spend some time finding a banker who will be part of your success team. The language of business is numbers, and numbers means money when we think of bankers. The banker is a critical member of your Success Team. Your banker needs to know your vision and your mission. You will need to give the banker your best pitch. The old saying—never go to a bank when you need money—is a half truth. If you find and build a sound relationship with a banker when you start your business, you may be able to obtain money even when you need it.

A banker is someone whom we can brainstorm with, bounce ideas off of, and get the latest thinking and trends on finance. We need someone who will work closely with us as the business grows. If you are like us, we always get a little nervous when we talk to the banker. So, it's important to find a banker who is intrigued with entrepreneurs and can relate to them.

Advisory Board

You will need to identify three to five advisors for your company. The advisors need to be successful businesspeople who welcome the opportunity to give you advice. They should be people who will give you their honest opinions and reactions to your business ideas. The advisors can be an informal group that can meet over dinner or in a formal meeting setting. We have had board meetings that were part of a Sunday Eagles football game, an overnight trip to the casinos in Atlantic City, or a dinner at our home.

The advisors should have different skills and expertise and have a relationship with you based on mutual respect. You probably need to meet at least twice a year and perhaps four times a year during the start-up phase of your business.

We recommend that you create a relationship with your local SBDC as part of your advisory team. There are over 1,000 SBDCs in the United States. You can find them by going to the Website of the Small Business Administration (www.sba.gov). They provide one-on-one free consulting for the entrepreneur and learning opportunities through low-cost workshops. The advisors can provide you with a sounding board for new ideas or initiatives that you wish to undertake.

In 1990, when Don's landscaping business had the opportunity to go into the business of constructing log homes, he sought the advice of an SBDC consultant. All four managers of the company thought it was a great idea. But when Don took it to the SBDC advisors, they smiled and said, "Are you crazy? We are in a recession. Home construction is not in your vision, nor is it the mission of the business. You will lose focus and you may bankrupt the business." Don didn't proceed with the venture and saved time and capital for his main business.

USING THE SUCCESS TEAM

The Success Team will help with everything from brainstorming to implementing. Get references on all of them before you choose them. Pick people who will listen to you but will not be afraid to tell you that you've got to get out of your Martian orbit and head back to Earth. Communicate your vision and make sure they understand what you're setting out to do. Listen to their advice but remember that though lawyers and accountants and other specialists are great advisors, it's you who is the entrepreneur. Their feedback and knowledge coupled with your energy, zeal, and creativity can make for a wonderfully productive team.

Also, make sure the people on your team can have fun and laugh. There will be plenty of times you'll need to do that!

STRATEGIC LEADERSHIP AND PUBLIC RELATIONS

There are two types of entrepreneurial leaders: those who want to stay in the background and lead from behind the scenes, and those who take their role public. Either way, the following tips will help you as a leader.

If you are the face of your company, part of your strategy should be managing your profile; how you come off as a leader. This item is not in the usual college course or training session because most people focus on the tasks of leadership and not the perception. Let's take a look at how this part of your plan can help propel you and your company toward the perception of attaining some degree of leadership.

First, perception without reality behind it won't help you hold any leadership position for long. What we're telling you here is that fact must back up perception.

- How you carry yourself says a lot about who you are.
- Do you exude confidence?
- Does your body language give the perception that you know what you're doing?
- Does your tone of voice make people want to listen and find out more?
- Do the words you choose compel others to look at you as a leader?
- Does the way you dress (which can be anything from jeans to expensive suits) project leadership?
- Do you model the behavior of a leader?
- Are you unique in your appearance in such a way as to make others want to take note of you without repelling them?

These things are all ingredients of your personal logo. That's right folks, just as your company has a logo, so do you.

Take note of the points above. Leaders know how to use those elements of communication to their advantage. In later chapters, we'll tell you how to execute these types of actions, along with other things to make your entrepreneurial leadership dreams come true, but for now, we'll give you some concrete examples of why the perception of leadership must be a part of your strategy.

A great personal logo and tag line along with substance make for an easier road to leadership. As we mentioned in a previous chapter, President Dwight Eisenhower's quote on leadership, "Leadership is the art of getting someone else to do something you want done because he [or she] wants to do it," allows us to think about what it is that enables great leaders to perfect that art. Eisenhower's words can provide us with some interesting conclusions. Read his words one more time and you will notice that it says nothing about the leader doing anything more than getting others to do what he or she wants. Certainly the fact that the former President helped lead the Allied Forces to victory in World War II gives whatever he speaks credence. His past performance is the substance while his words and the image of the man reflect his logo.

Leaders who can give people confidence through their look, body language, tone of voice, compelling words, and deeds know that their persona is as much a part of their leadership strategy as any other business item on their strategic agenda.

The media is drawn to entrepreneurial leaders who have their personal logos and those of their company well defined. Because public relations should be a major part of any business's strategy, having a message that can be conveyed with confidence, strength, and innovation is something most newspapers, magazines, television and radio stations, and the new media will have a hard time ignoring.

How often have you heard people speak about a leader at their place of employment or other venue and, when you make their acquaintance, you understand why? It's because of their personal logo.

An entrepreneur who is trying to sell his or her ideas to family, friends, their bank, venture capitalists, their customers, vendors, and employees is partially, if not entirely, judged by their personal logo.

Bill Gates has the persona you would expect for his type of business. Perhaps too much flash wouldn't have worked for him. Donald Trump, on the other hand, fits right into the swashbuckling real estate tycoon mold. Ben and Jerry are perfect examples of entrepreneurial leaders whose hippie looks go right along with what they sell. The list can go on forever. You may be thinking of some of your entrepreneurial leadership heroes who fit the bill right now. The personal logo doesn't apply 100% of the time, but, on average, we'd say you're better off perfecting yours than not.

STAY THE COURSE

You can see that as we've taken you from understanding your mission to getting your strategy in place there has to be a certain consistency in whatever it is you do. Changing focus can be fatal, especially for the early-stage entrepreneur. Later in the entrepreneurial cycle, changing focus can actually help the entrepreneurial leader take advantage of new opportunities as we will see further along in this book. For now, however, creating a well-defined course and staying it will ensure a better chance of success.

Your vision, mission, and strategy all have to layer over each other in such a way as to instill the confidence that your stakeholders will need for them to buy from you, invest in you, refer to you, and work for you.

The brand you set out to display to the world, a subject we will also cover in greater depth later, is everything you have, wrapped up in a nutshell. You are its symbol, your company its body, your philosophy its soul. Having a strategy that understands those issues and can implement them through a well-determined action plan with proper execution can lead you and your enterprise into the business world well prepared for the competitive environment you are sure to face.

KEY POINTS AND LESSONS LEARNED

☑ Your mission implements your vision. It puts dimensions on your dream.
☑ Write your three strategic thrusts on a 4″ x 6″ index card.
☑ What information do you need to know to expedite the execution of your mission? Make those professionals part of your Success Team.
☑ Perception really is reality.
☑ Your personal logo should fit the industry and your company's position in it.
☑ Write your strategic intent statement and share it with your stakeholders.
☑ Vision > Mission > Strategy.

Your Action Plan and Execution

Welcome to the land of action! This is the step where you begin to reveal your leadership capabilities to the outside world. You've done quite a few things up to this point. Let's do a quick review of what you've learned so far:

You now know how important a leadership model is for you and your business. It is the foundation upon which all the other elements rest.

You've learned about yourself, you understand your behaviors, attitudes, value system, ethical framework, and other factors that make you who you are. And you learned how those factors affect your business and your relationships with people around you.

You've acquired insights into what motivates you and what passions move you forward. You know how others become motivated, why they are passionate about certain things, and you've learned that two people can reach the same goal by taking different paths and do it for different reasons.

You've seen how your vision for your business can set the groundwork for what you see your business becoming. You've seen how your passion is the fuel that compels you to act. It's the driving force behind accomplishing what you do.

You've attained knowledge of how your business mission can give you the tools to move your vision into reality. Now, you know how your strategy can take those tools and create a plan to take the steps needed to fulfill your business dreams.

You've seen the requirement to develop three strategies that you will focus on and execute to achieve excellence.

You have moved to fulfill the six As (which includes four of the core members of your success team):

1. Acquire a name
2. Analyze your expenses and revenue projections
3. Accountant has been brought on board
4. Attorney has been added to your team
5. Artist has been hired to do your graphics and promotion materials
6. Advisors have been identified.

Figure 5.1
Leadership Model—Your Action Plan and Execution

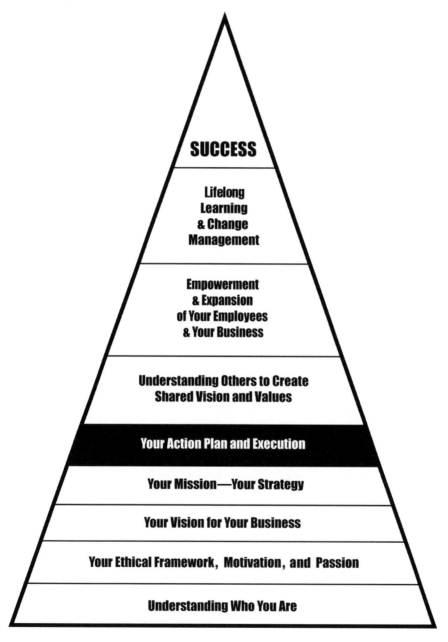

SUCCESS

Lifelong
Learning
& Change
Management

Empowerment
& Expansion
of Your Employees
& Your Business

Understanding Others to Create
Shared Vision and Values

Your Action Plan and Execution

Your Mission—Your Strategy

Your Vision for Your Business

Your Ethical Framework, Motivation, and Passion

Understanding Who You Are

With all that accomplished, you now have the ability to move ahead into the action arena with a clear understanding of what you intend to do, how you intend to do it, and with whom you intend to do it. You are ready for action planning.

THE SEVEN-STEP ACTION PLAN

Your action plan and the execution of that plan will allow you to begin to see the results of your labors. Action planning allows you to execute your mission and to move toward reaching your vision. The planning process and the actual experience of planning are critical to the entrepreneurial leader.

Writing your action plan is a process of discovery: It allows you to communicate with your key employees and stakeholders. That period of planning and the exchanging of ideas can be a creative and fun experience for everyone involved. This process helps you get the participants' buy-in. As Dr. Graeme Edwards has said, "It's not the plan that is important, it's the planning."

The plan does not have to be a long document but must be written. The seven components of the action plan are Vision, Mission, Goals, Objectives, Strategy, Plan, and Activities.

For many years Don has utilized this seven-step action plan in working with large corporations as well as numerous small businesses.

So far, we've worked with you to create your vision, we've helped you to define your mission, and we've assisted you in creating your strategy. Now, we will integrate these three components into the Seven-Step Action Plan.

1. *Vision.* It is critical during the building of an action plan that everyone involved in the process has a clear understanding of your vision and your timeframe. Your vision, including your mental picture of your vision and your written vision statement, will serve as inspiration for the planning process. You and your employees need to understand the passion (fuel) that drives the enterprise.
2. *Mission.* As you begin to build your action plan, keep your mission statement in front of you and your employees. Your mission statement should be your guide to executing a meaningful plan and, as we discussed in the previous chapter, it should guide you as you transition your vision into reality. You must stay focused on your mission as you build your plan.
3. *Goals.* You need to develop clearly written, measurable goals. The goals should be one year in length. They must lead toward the vision and the execution of the mission of the business. Without measurable goals you have no promises to keep or challenges to face.
4. *Objectives.* You need to develop quarterly objectives that will help you achieve your yearly goals and move you toward the attainment of your vision. These objectives should be written and should enable you to see movement toward your vision and mission.

5. *Strategy*. You need to develop the three key strategies (discussed in the previous chapter) that will lead you to business success as well as the achievement of your vision. This is the most challenging part of building an action plan. Your strategies will drive your actions. The current business climate may demand that you seek out strategic partners to help execute the mission and keep your costs low.

6. *Plan*. You need to develop a monthly plan that will help you reach your quarterly objectives. This might be a one pager that you write at the beginning of the month that prioritizes the most important action items for that month. You have to hold yourself accountable to stay focused on your key strategies and objectives.

7. *Activities*. The activities are daily and weekly. You should select a system that works for you, such as a to-do list or a computer schedule. If you stand back and look at how you manage your time on a daily and weekly basis, you should see that the majority of your time is devoted to achieving your monthly, quarterly, and yearly goals and objectives. Prioritize your daily to-do lists and make sure you start with the top-rated items.

This process is logical and easy to follow once you have a clear vision and mission. The planning process is difficult for entrepreneurs. You may have to struggle to allocate the time to do it. The rewards are great, however, and should give you an extra dose of confidence.

Review your vision and mission, translate them into goals and objectives, and formulate a strategy to reach those desired results. Dan's example of how he grew For Eyes may be a good road map for your enterprise. Come up with a strategy based on your vision and mission, put it into practice, infuse some advertising, institute a public relations program, hire great employees, and modify your plan based on the outcome.

Sir John Harvey-Jones said, "Planning is an unnatural process; it is much more fun to do something. The nicest thing about not planning is that failure comes as a complete surprise, rather than being preceded by a period of worry and depression."

THE ROLE OF THE SUCCESS TEAM IN PLANNING

As noted in the previous chapter, whether you're working from your home, a shop, or an outside office, you should start to build your Success Team. Your lawyer will set up your business entity either as a sole proprietorship, partnership, Limited Liability Company, C-Corporation, S-Corporation, or other type of enterprise. As your business grows, you will have your lawyer review contracts and assist in contract negotiation. Your lawyer should be part of the planning process as well as a confidential advisor.

You and your accountant will establish a fiscal year end, develop revenue and expense reporting systems, and review other tax issues. You should plan to meet with your accountant on a regular basis to be mentored in all aspects of finance and accounting as it relates to your business. During the planning process your accountant can help with critical financial forecasts.

Your graphic artist/marketing communication specialist (with your input) will design your logo, letterhead, envelope, and business card. Your Webmaster will build version 1.0 of your Website. The Webmaster is a required member of your Success Team and your planning team. During the planning process, the Webmaster and marketing communication specialist can prepare marketing ideas as well as help identify the latest trends for the team to review. Also, you need to involve your banker. The Success Team enables you to head out into the world to implement your business strategies, follow through on your mission, and make your vision a reality.

GETTING CUSTOMERS

What's next? Getting people to buy what you're selling sounds like a good start. The question is: how do you do that? It all starts with you. You are the face of your business, and by definition you are the number one salesperson. This is the time for you to lead people to your door, Website, phone number, or whatever vehicle becomes the best prospect or client "touch point."

By building an action plan, you begin to formulate the means by which your business will position itself for growth. Take a look at the money that you've allocated for your monthly sales and marketing effort. It may be quite a bit or it may be zilch, nada, nothing.

Look at the resources you have at your disposal. It may come down to you, your business cards, and your Website. Having a good artist/marketing communication person on your Success Team is essential. As you may have surmised, we are bootstrap-type of people, and it's common for us to start a new venture with the same bankroll that you may have: zero.

Whether you've created a retail business or a service business, there are ways to begin the process of letting people know that your new company exists by using very little monetary outlay on your part. It's called using your mouth. Telling people what you do in a succinct way is an effective means of finding new prospects and clients.

First decide who or what your target market is. Then work on finding out where they exist. For instance, determine what size companies you'd like to have as clients. Are you looking to go after large corporations and institutions or small businesses and organizations? These are two distinctly different markets. However, that doesn't mean that you won't accept businesses in one, even if you've targeted the other (more on that later), but for now let's choose one. For purposes of illustration, we'll assume that small business is where you'd like to become a player.

SUCCESS CONNECTIONS/NETWORKING PROCESS

Networking is an inexpensive and effective way to begin positioning your company as one that offers something worth buying. You will be doing a lot of networking and speaking with many people in various locations and in different settings where potential clients may be (including everything from your local supermarket or grocery store to the local neighborhood civic council, to the area and/or regional Chambers of Commerce, to specialized industry membership associations, etc.). Your job right now is to find all the small-business people and outlets that will need what you're selling. That means getting on the Internet and using search engines to figure out where they exist. You can also use the phone book, the white and yellow pages, to uncover the jewels you may be looking for.

When you are mining the small-business market, your chances of being able to speak with the owner and/or decision-maker are greater than if you target a vice president for IBM. That doesn't mean that you'll be able to get through every time, just that your chances are better. The probability of finding a person of influence from a major company attending the events or in the venues mentioned above is small.

Next, lay out a networking plan of action that describes how you will reach these groups and the people within them. Perhaps it means attending meetings on your own, volunteering to be a speaker (possibly in exchange for a membership), becoming a student at some free classes, or joining a friend who already is a member as their guest. Don made it a practice to speak at property management meetings about "Trends in Landscape Management." This gave him the opportunity to talk to managers about environmentally safe practices. Within three years, the majority of his business was with property management companies.

Always, no matter where you are or what you're doing, carry your business cards with you. You never know when you'll need them! Once you have your schedule as to what events you will attend, think about the opportunities that lie within each group. Does "Group A" have committees (a fact you should have been able to ascertain by viewing their Website or making a phone call to their offices)? Is "Group B" attended by only owners or does it have managers as well? Is "Group C" filled with people of influence within the community? Getting prepared for your networking meetings always enables you to know what you'll be confronting.

The networking scenario that we just described can be achieved whether you do or do not have money to spend on other forms of marketing. Either way, it's one of the best action steps to position your business for success. It also holds true for entrepreneurs who are just starting out or who have a solid ongoing business. The way you interact with others when you are networking will be viewed by others, including your employees, as a mark of confidence and leadership. So, take heed to sharpen your networking skills and techniques. As we mentioned in Chapter 4, your networking abilities help build your personal image and that of your enterprise.

One of the best networking professionals we know is a lawyer who is a master of observation. He studies the attendees at functions, watches their body language, listens to their tonality, and the topics of their discussions. He takes note of what they drink and eat. From that enhanced perspective, he's ready to make whomever he decides to approach feel comfortable. Using his knowledge of communication, he will start conversations about subjects they have already shown an interest in. He will stand the way they do, speak with them in a tone that closely matches theirs, and ask them probing questions in ways that make his discussion partner feel at ease. Then, of course, he listens. It may sound simple, yet it's not very common. Needless to say, his practice does quite well.

Another thing our lawyer friend is very good at is making sure the functions he attends have the right demographic for his practice, which focuses on small-business start-ups and venture-funded organizations. You won't see him going to networking events where the attendees are all larger corporation middle- and upper-level executives, unless they include venture fund managers or other individuals who can send him referrals.

He sits on committees in the four organizations to which he belongs. Over the years, he has positioned himself to be viewed as a leader in his field and the lawyer of choice for his target market.

We have spoken with him many times, and he is adamant about sticking to his action plan and staying with its execution. It has worked out extremely well for him. His vision was to be known as the small-business and venture-funded expert in the region, his mission was to help small businesses and venture-funded companies grow and prosper by using his expertise and those in his firm while also treating his clients with respect, fairness, and quick responsiveness. His key strategy was to be seen and heard as often as possible by his target market so as to be recognized as the expert his vision so clearly outlined.

THE 30-SECOND PITCH AND ACTIVE LISTENING

A "pitch" is a 30-second explanation that communicates to others what you are all about. Plan on writing a pitch that captures the essence and passion of everything you do in about 30 seconds. Make it such that it solves a problem that the person you're speaking with may have or know someone who has. The pitch must make an emotional connection with the customer and answer the customer's question, "So what?" In other words, your pitch must be the benefits, not the features, of your product or service.

Let's pretend that you've just started a business transporting elderly patients to doctor's offices. You've just arrived at a networking event of a local businesspersons' association of your community. Soon, you start strolling throughout the restaurant in which the meeting is held. Your body language and tone of voice exude leadership. You may feel a bit of anxiety or fear, but you must remember that being an entrepreneurial leader means taking risks and risks entail going outside of your comfort zone and into the unknown. If it were easy, everyone would be doing it. Mentally focus on your passion, and it will give you the motivation and energy to enjoy the situation. The beauty of what you're encountering is that you've planned for it.

You're now fully engaged in the usual chitchat that happens at networking events when your conversation partner asks what you do. The 30-second pitch you've prepared comes effortlessly out of your mouth. "We help elderly people get to their appointments without putting pressure on themselves, their children, or their other caregivers. We pick them up, transport them to and within the facilities where they're visiting, wait for them, and then take them back home. With care and compassion, we make their lives easier and relieve their stress and worry. You wouldn't know anyone who needs our service would you?"

You've just read a 30-second spot that should get a positive response from lots of people. You're solving a problem that a lot of people have without saying that you're the best thing around. Your objective is to get a response and get leads. By listening to people, you will get information you may not have dreamed of. Although the person you're speaking with may not need your service, the chances of that person knowing someone who does is pretty good. Because we live in a listening-deprived society, people who ask questions and listen, really listen, to the answer will always be respected and liked.

This is also where you exchange business cards and show off that beautiful logo on impressive card stock along with your attention-getting, easy-to-remember, business name and Web site.

The combination of the pitch and actively listening will help your business grow. This combination must be a major part of your action plan and execution tactics. If you ask the right questions and listen to the answers, your client base will tell you everything you need to know. It's a simple premise, but too many entrepreneurs don't heed it. Leaders find out what other people know, and then they take action based on that knowledge.

A person who becomes an excellent listener is also a person that other people will want to talk with. People enjoy being around people who take an interest in them. The easy way to show that is to listen. The more you cultivate that skill, the more your potential clients will want to speak with you. Many experts on leadership consider listening as the single greatest skill an entrepreneur can acquire. There's the added value of being told what's causing a person's problems that you may have the solution for!

In the last few words of your 30-second spot, ask for something that is invaluable: a referral. Referrals are a wonderful way to build a solid business, yet so many people are afraid to ask for them.

Out of a feeling of trust, leaders get people to do what they want them to do because the people want to do it. It is the backbone of any solid relationship. Successful leaders know that once they've built a level of trust with someone, which can happen over time or immediately, they are more apt to get what they want done. Listening builds trust.

AN ACTION PLAN EXAMPLE

Let's share some insights from Dan on the action plan for his optical company. For Eyes' strategy was to produce the best quality eyewear by buying from vendors whose products he trusted; to provide superb service by using the latest, best performing, and most efficient equipment; and to charge the lowest possible prices by keeping his overhead and personal financial needs to a minimum. It all sounds like a winning combination, but it wouldn't have happened if he didn't have a plan and the skills and tactics to make it work.

First, he called all of his preferred suppliers and explained his plan. Dan didn't have a lot of money and would need credit and longer payment terms. Because he knew them, the suppliers gave him what he asked with some restrictions. For instance, he could get extended terms on the original orders of frames and lenses, but all orders after the initial ones would be paid according to normal terms.

Dan used outside laboratories at the beginning of the venture to defray upfront equipment costs. Many entrepreneurs use this tactic to help lower capital expenditures. Sometimes these businesses never purchase equipment and remain distribution/marketing companies. By outsourcing all their production, they leave that entire area up to their strategic partners who are, in essence, their vendors. Dan would, however, check into the factories to see what type of equipment they were using and what their return and accuracy rates were.

He then used projections to determine price structure. Once the action plan was in place and all the elements were ready to go, he executed the plan. Frames and lenses arrived (along with their extended term invoices). Frames were displayed on pushpins that were stuck into pegboard. His used furniture was in place (low overhead), and the doors were opened.

Of course, he now had to get customers into the store, anyone with eyes needing correction. He started by focusing on students. The original store was in Center City Philadelphia behind the Philadelphia College of Art, around the corner from Pierce Junior College, walking distance or a short bus ride from the University of Pennsylvania, a fifteen-minute subway trip from Temple University, and a six-block walk from the Community College of Philadelphia and Thomas Jefferson University. Dan reasoned that students would understand his pricing policy and look to take advantage of it because the vast majority of them were constrained monetarily. He also was fully aware that they would feel extremely comfortable within the store's "funky" environment because most of them lived in the same conditions. Finally, he knew that they would relate easily to his long hair and tee-shirt appearance because they looked the same.

Dan's meager advertising took the form of cartoon display ads in campus newspapers. They worked. He knew his market. Within six months, he was able to bring many of the laboratory functions in-house, which ensured the ability to have an even quicker turnaround and better quality. These aspects led to even more business, and the cycle continued until all manufacturing was taken over by a now larger, wholly owned laboratory facility that also housed a frame-importing company and a store furniture manufacturing plant. Every growth spurt called for updated plans and revised execution strategies.

Other elements that helped Dan's business grow quickly were the use of public relations, marketing, and promotions. Your personal and corporate logos can go a long way to make you the leader in your field. Ben and Jerry's ice cream conjures up the picture of the two men who started the company as well as their beautifully and humorously designed packages. We see both of those images in our minds because of their exposure in the media, the placement in our grocery stores, and their promotional items and events in our society. There is no doubt that if you walk up to a large portion of the population of the United States and ask them to name the two men who are the entrepreneurial leaders in ice-cream products, a vast majority would say Ben and Jerry.

Is it an accident? I don't think so. Our two ice-cream tycoons along with many of our other entrepreneurial leadership icons have something in common: their personal and business logos. Each executed splendidly.

Dan's experience of being in major newspapers, magazines, and on television and radio was achieved at first by accident (if you discount the uniqueness of his service), but he quickly realized that by using that uniqueness and his communications skills and strengths of his logos he could expand his entrepreneurial leadership role greatly.

Part of your action plan should be how you will address public relations. Figure out what your unique entrepreneurial proposition is and perfect it. Tell the world about who you are and what you do. Plan it out and then execute.

The execution of that plan section will include sending out your stories to publications and online article directories (a list of article directories is easily accessible on Google). The key to getting attention is doing something so unique that media outlets will come to you. The trick to keeping attention is to avoid being sales oriented. Be informative instead. The audience will get the message. You may even consider hiring a public relations firm or public relations freelancer. Speak at functions related to your field. Again, be aware of overselling in your speeches. People will want to listen to you if they feel that you're authentic, honest, and not doing a hard sell.

Your action plan should include other elements as well. Keep your name in front of your target market. Promotional items can do this for you. It helps to make the look of your items unique, whether that means unusual shaped mugs, leather-bound books with your logo, different styles of hats, or whatever you feel will make you stand out. There are promotional experts to help you with the process.

The last item on the marketing side of the action plan is advertising. A word of caution: you can lose a lot of money fast by throwing your dollars at advertising. Spend lots of time researching the different advertising venues and ask for their media kits. Once you open the doors of your entre-preneurial endeavor, you will be besieged by people who will want you to advertise in or on their media outlets. Consider value carefully.

The best type of advertising for the highly targeted entrepreneur is direct marketing. There are a number of superb companies doing fantastic things such as consumer personalized postcards that link to tracking Websites, which, in turn, give you reports as to who has viewed your postcards and looked at the Website indicated on the card, or called the toll-free number that is answered at the direct marketing company. As intricate as this process sounds, it is not overly expensive and usually pays for itself and more. Remember, each time your card reaches the home or business of your target market it is one more impression that's been made on the recipient's mind.

Being recognized as a leader is as much about perception as reality. The more impressions you can make on your customer, the easier it is for them to perceive your leadership status. Of course, the perception of leadership can melt away very quickly if you don't perform like a leader. Be prepared to service what you sell, respond to your customers' needs, give that extra effort, and display the leadership qualities that will ensure that, in your case, perception is indeed reality!

ACTION PLAN AND FINDING GOOD EMPLOYEES

When you plan for growth, you inevitably will be faced with the deci-sion to stay small, which may mean a one-person business, or you may decide to grow outside of your own capabilities, which will mean hiring employees. How you deal with employees once they're on board is an important subject, which we will get into in depth in the next chapter. However, we can certainly discuss the planning aspect of finding capable help in this one.

Understanding who you are and what you do well will enable you to realize what types of positions you need to fill. Finding the employees you want to hire can be difficult. Knowing that skill levels, knowledge, work ethics, and other important factors compose the requirements for the vari-ous jobs within your organization makes it clear that attracting good people is as important as going out and finding them. That fact alone makes build-ing your personal logo and the image of your company an aspect that will help you attract, hire, and retain desirable folks.

When people recognize your brand and read about you and your company in a positive light, they will want to work for you. Entrepreneurial leaders who spend time establishing their company's identity as well as their own seem to spend less time looking for capable employees than those who don't. The job market is tough. Many entrepreneurs are having a diffi-cult time filling important slots. Your company's image affects various aspects of your growth plan, each of which can make it easier to achieve your goals.

If your organization hasn't yet had the exposure needed to get the attention of job seekers, there are other ways to find the people you need. Even if you have begun to build the exposure and company identity you desire, having alternative resources in your action plan can help. The list below can assist you in searching out a range of new hires, whether you're looking for upper level managers, technicians, hourly laborers, subcontractors, freelancers, or any other type:

- Speak with placement centers at universities, trade schools, and other educational institutions to help you promote your company and the positions you have available. They will often post your job listings and discuss them with people they counsel.
- Contact your local workforce development office. These organizations help cultivate people, through training programs, so they can become assets to the local business community. Most cities and regions have a workforce development office although they may go under different names in some areas.
- Jobs fairs are wonderful places to find good people. Whether your company chooses to be an exhibitor or you decide to "walk the floor" and speak with attendees, these events are filled with people looking for jobs!
- The Internet has become a superb place to post job listings and look at résumés. Sites like Monster.com and CareerBuilder.com have become extremely popular destinations for jobs seekers and employers. There may be subscription costs involved, so check the Website's terms.
- Houses of worship and community centers usually have a pretty good idea who in their area is in need of a job. Plus, you have the advantage of asking people within those organizations about the individuals who are recommended. You can consider that a bit of a prescreening process.
- Outplacement centers are enterprises that help folks who have been laid off to work on their existing skills, hone new skills, take training classes, write résumés, and perform other services to make it easier for them to reenter the workforce. The attendees' former companies pay many of these organizations as part of a severance package.
- Organizations that cater to the physically and mentally challenged are great resources to acquire employees who have been trained in specific job skills. Their managers know what participants' capabilities are and sculpt their programs to match them.
- Employment agencies and "headhunter" firms are paid by the eventual employer to find specifically qualified individuals. Most will screen candidates before sending you their résumés. If you choose a person from their pool of folks, you will be responsible for compensating the agency. Fees range in the area of 30% of the new employee's first year's salary. But remember, they've done a lot of the searching and prescreening for you.
- Trade publication classified advertising is a super way to find people in your industry. Most people who read your industry's trade publications

are already in your field and probably have some, if not all, of the skills you're looking for. These people may want to work for you as an employee or work with you as a subcontractor or freelancer.

- Newspaper and magazine classified ads have been done for years and years and still seem to work. Although you may have to go through quite a few people to get to one who really has the skills you're looking for, it may still be worth the effort.
- Some government programs will compensate employers for training people who are reentering the workforce or who need to be retrained to gain employment. This compensation can vary, but it may mean that, during the on-the-job training period, the government agency will pay for all or a sizable portion of the trainee's salary. Sometimes, there may be a period after the training when the employer still receives reimbursement for some percentage of the employee's salary. Call your local, regional, and/or state government to see if they have such programs. The workforce development center may also help you in this area. Perhaps, they may even be a participating agency.

By using the entities listed above along with some of the resources in Appendix A, you can make adding employees a little easier. Hiring the right people will enhance your entrepreneurial growth. Your leadership skills will also be tested as you now move forward with your endeavor and work with others who will, hopefully, want to do things that you want them to do because they want to do them! In the next chapter, we'll show you how to create an atmosphere that will, indeed, make that possible.

By putting hiring, or acquiring, the right talent into your action plan and taking the necessary steps to execute it, you will take some of the stress out of your organization's expansion.

KEY POINTS AND LESSONS LEARNED

- ☑ Action Planning is the list of steps you must take to make your plan real.
- ☑ Doing the six As will start to build your Success Team.
- ☑ Set up your company's legal structure and design your business image.
- ☑ Networking is inexpensive but powerful in getting the word out. Focus on the group of your highest potential customers, called your target market.
- ☑ Prepare your 30-second pitch. Say what you do to benefit customers and ask for a referral.
- ☑ Figure out what makes you and your company unique, then tell the world.
- ☑ Like-minded employees are attracted by the image of your company.
- ☑ Vision > Mission > Goals > Objectives > Strategy > Plan > Activities.

Understanding Others to Create Shared Vision and Values

So, here we are: vision in hand, mission on board, strategy laid out, action plan understood, and execution begun. Now what? We will present two in-depth case studies that guide you through the process of understanding others and creating the shared vision that allowed us to succeed in our business endeavors and will give you a process for your enterprise.

Before you head out into the world of commerce once again, take a few minutes and think about how you're going to go about sharing the concept of what you do with others. We know that we discussed some of this in Chapter 5, as it related to your elevator speech and networking, but here we're tackling something deeper.

Although your company may be selling the most innovative products or compelling service, there's another element that many entrepreneurs forget about: understanding others. Understanding others separates the wheat from the chaff, the men from the boys, the women from the girls, the cream from the milk, and the leaders from the regular folks. It is also what makes people buy into what you are doing and selling, and keeps them coming back for more.

Shared vision and values are also important. Huh? Didn't we go over vision and values? Well yes, we did, except, now, we're going to take it to the next level using case studies.

The first of the two case studies is about Elmer, a potential customer of your software development firm. Elmer's story is one every salesperson and entrepreneur can identify with. As you read the case study, think through how you currently share your values, mission, and vision with your employees and all other stakeholders.

So, put on your shoes (or sneakers) and get ready to take a walk a bit further down the Entrepreneurial Leadership road.

CASE STUDY: THE STORY OF ELMER

Ah, what a beautiful day it is today. The perfect time to start to understand what it takes to get customers, clients, and employees to jump on

Figure 6.1
Leadership Model—Understanding Others to Create Shared Vision and Values

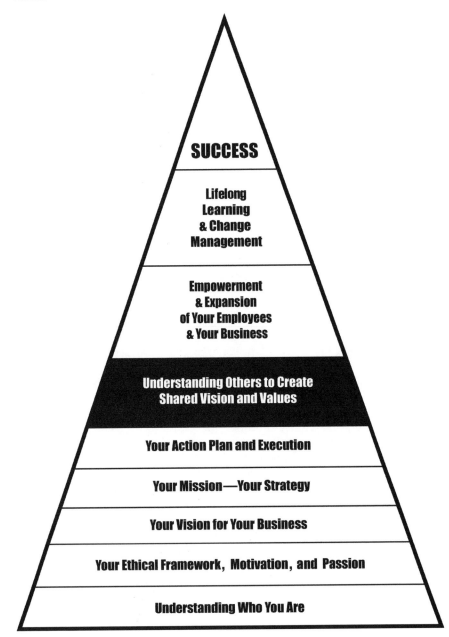

board your entrepreneurial software enterprise experiment and stay there for a long time!

As we travel down the road, to our right, we see a potential customer (because practically everyone is a potential customer) sitting on the emerald grass of a park enjoying the bright sunshine and cool breeze. We stop and chat. Soon, we're chums and calling each other by our first names (because you knew how to listen and network from the last chapter). Your new friend, Elmer, starts to fill you in on his life. You find out that he works for a major company in town, Big Steve's Wholesale Furniture Outlet. Big Steve has five huge stores in your city alone. Not to mention the 35 others spread around the county. You recognize the business success of Big Steve's. You begin to ask Elmer how things are going and listen intently to his answers. Each pearl that comes out of his mouth you store away for future reference.

You're beginning to have a clearer picture of what really goes on behind the scenes at Big Steve's as well as what's happening in Elmer's life.

You are looking for what motivates Elmer, because you know that what motivates him is what counts. You want to connect with each person you wish to either buy from you or work for you. As you've learned, each person is motivated by different things and behaves in different ways. But you can form a common ground and share common visions and values because underneath we all want the same things.

Back to Elmer who has told you his entire life's story and enabled you to realize that he's an "effusive" person who is motivated by knowledge and by getting a return on his investment. He's even related his ethical ideals to you. By those simple facts, you are now gaining the upper hand in understanding others as well as what it will take to get them to buy what you're selling.

In his story, Elmer relates the fact that he's become frustrated with how long it takes to get prospects and customers to make up their minds. You ask Elmer why, and he tells you that he believes that they want to check out other furniture stores before making a decision. You ask him how good he is at getting information from prospects and customers, and he says that he tries, but people seem to be hesitant. You suggest to Elmer that perhaps it may be a good idea to find out how many other shops his prospects have been to before visiting Big Steve's. Your next question is, "If you had all the resources available to you to help you keep in touch with prospects and customers, what would it look like?" We can just about guarantee that he'll give you the answer.

Once you have his answer in hand, you continue to dig even deeper. Asking how long he's had the problem, does he think that others within his organization have the same situations, and how much money is it costing him and the company.

You then state to Elmer that, if you could help him relieve his problems, does he think that it would be worthwhile to visit him at work? He gives you a positive response (a negative one would have been okay too), you exchange numbers, set up a time to speak, find out if he is the decision-maker or not (and, if not, ask how you could include the person who will ultimately make the decision in your meeting), thank your new friend, and say good-bye. You now have a relatively clear understanding of Elmer's behavior, values, frustrations, motivators, decision-making capabilities, and other factors that you can use to create a solution that will take care of his angst.

After taking in your last glorious view of the greenery, you leave the beautiful park and make your way back to your office. Firmly seated at your desk you begin to craft your thoughts on paper. A series of questions comes to mind:

- How will I *create a feeling* that will make Elmer understand how and why I can help him?
- How can I *relate to his value system* while still being true to mine?
- How can I *instill the vision* I have for my company relative to his organization?

We know that people buy based on emotion. Tapping into Elmer's emotions is key to getting your new client.

By reviewing all the points Elmer related to you and integrating them with the vision and mission of your company, you start to lay out a strategy to help Big Steve's eliminate their problem. You rehash Elmer's emotions and the facts he's passed your way and recognize some very important issues that your software company may be able to solve. First you look at your software company's vision and mission statements.

Your vision is: To build a cutting-edge, high-growth, innovative, and profitable software development company that works with clients to help them resolve problems, create growth, and build prosperity and profitability.

Your tag line is: We take you to the cutting edge of technology at the most productive level.

Your mission is: To bring the latest technological solutions to our clients by connecting to their values, vision, mission, and goals while adding the human interaction that will help us design the technology, systems, and processes to enhance our company and those of our clients. We will provide our service responsibly, quickly, proactively, and with our client's best interests in mind.

Next, you think about whether or not your company can design the type of software that Big Steve's needs, or if you currently have the technology in place that may help them immediately. If you cannot or do not have the capability or availability of either, you must think about your ethics and values and decide to pass on Big Steve's rather than stringing Elmer along or creating ill will. If you do pass on the opportunity, it would be a good idea to also let Elmer know which company you believe will be able to fulfill his needs. You should make sure that you explain why you won't be able to help him and exactly where your expertise lies. That act alone will help you with referrals in the future.

But let's say you're going to be able to work with Elmer and Big Steve's. Empathy for what Elmer's going through is the best way to start your relationship. Buying into his problem will ensure you that you're both on the same page. Most prospects can see that quality in an entrepreneur and appreciate his or her willingness to take the time to delve into their situation. The more you listen, the more you learn, the easier it is to lead.

In your meeting with Elmer and perhaps the other decision maker, make sure you bring questions that may add to the information you've already compiled. It's also advisable to tell Elmer to do the same. This can be done when you call Elmer to confirm the meeting. In addition to letting Elmer know that he should think about what he may want or need, he's also getting the picture that you care about him and his company's vision and values.

It's no surprise that, when Dan started his optical company, he realized that most people were experiencing the same problem—being charged high prices for a necessity with no alternatives. With that in mind, he set about starting something that would create a vision everyone could easily share and a value system that others could buy into as well. He did that through his ability to listen to his potential customers, asking others how they felt about his idea, and letting his intuition guide him without overtaking reason. He stayed true to his values, vision, motivators, passion, and mission. Most entrepreneurial leaders have an overriding confidence that comes with the understanding that they will succeed as long as they persevere and do not stray too much from their vision and mission.

Thomas Edison said, "Opportunity is missed by most people because it is dressed as overalls and looks like work."

Entrepreneurial leaders know how to spot the opportunities even if they are dressed in overalls. That's why they'll listen to the likes of Elmer and work on understanding them. Entrepreneurs will also spend a great deal of time devising a method of creating a shared vision and values that reflect those of their prospects and clients as well.

In the second case study, we will walk you through the process of building a shared vision based on an understanding of the client and the importance of building a custom solution to the client's problem.

CASE STUDY: SATURN PROJECT, WILMINGTON, DELAWARE, 1996

Don founded PICE Inc. with a partner in 1996. When Don returned to the General Motors' (GM) Wilmington Assembly plant with his new company, the plant was in turmoil. He realized that this was a critical moment in the history of the plant. The plant needed to move to the team concept to keep its doors open. GM and the United Auto Workers (UAW) had signed an agreement to transition to a team concept at the facility and, in return, the plant would build the Chevy Malibu while also transitioning to build one of the Saturn models. This agreement would guarantee the existence and the future for the plant. But "Teaming" was a whole new vision for the UAW and GM in Wilmington.

The first contract for PICE Inc. was for $8,000 to design and develop a training program. Don spent a lot of time on-site during the development phase of the program listening to the concerns of both the GM managers and the UAW. One GM manager kept asking Don, "Why are you spending so much time on a small contract?" Don answered, "I want to understand how your concerns fit into the new team concept and to get it right the first time."

No one was sure about implementing the team concept in an old manufacturing site with a long history of union and management antagonism. The longer Don listened to the client, however, the more it became clear that the vision and mission of PICE could align with the vision and values of the GM plant. Einstein's quote says it so well. "It's not that I'm so smart, it's just that I stay with a problem longer." With perseverance and hard work, the shared vision became so apparent to all involved that the relationship grew into a half-million-dollar contract. This team building project would provide 95% of PICE's revenue over the following year.

The process that Don used in 1996 with GM at the Wilmington Assembly Plant had to build shared vision and values with GM, Saturn, all of PICE's subcontractors, and, most important of all, the employees of the Wilmington, Delaware, facility. Their task was to design, develop and deliver a four-day, cofacilitated, team-building learning experience for all employees of the facility. They would accomplish this task over a four-month period by initially delivering the workshop on first and second shifts and then, ultimately, on the third shift.

Don and his partner needed to locate 30 top-quality facilitators who had expertise in team building—and they had to do it in 30 days. They had to find them, interview them, put them under contract, and train them. To help them locate the facilitators, they reached out to some key organizations in the Philadelphia area.

When they interviewed them, they ascertained whether or not the interviewees shared the same vision as PICE and GM. For example, if Don noted, "You will need to be available to help us on two shifts," and the interviewee answered, "I never work the second shift," Don's answer was, "You won't be working here!" The assembly plant worked on three shifts. The shared vision did not include facilitators whose attitude might be interpreted as "class superiority."

The facilitators also needed to be team players. If Don noted, "To accomplish a powerful team-building workshop, our design calls for it to be cofacilitated. What do you think?" and the response he received was, "I have a Ph.D. and certainly don't need help." Don's response was, "Not to worry, you won't be working with us on this project." The facilitators needed to model teamwork, including the acceptance of cofacilitation and a willingness to work all shifts, to demonstrate the shared vision.

To ensure a consistent vision, after hiring the 30 subcontractors, the next step in our process was to instill in them the shared vision and values. That required all facilitators to observe the four-day team-building program. This was followed by the facilitators cofacilitating a four-day workshop that then led to them becoming the lead facilitator in a four-day program. This rigorous process inculcated the team concept at the facilitation level and, most important, provided the learning experience to management and labor in those workshops.

PICE spent a great deal of time and money to standardize the materials used in all workshops. They wanted consistent delivery and emphasis on the skills necessary to successfully implement the team concept at Wilmington. The workshops were based on adult learning theory that places a premium on the active participation of all those involved in the workshops. Their quality assurance process focused on evaluating each program for its consistency and its impact on workers.

A shared vision also requires leaders to make a very strong, powerful statement followed by some tangible, concrete demonstration supporting the vision. The plant leadership at Wilmington gave up their executive car garage. GM converted the space and built a state-of-the-art learning center for Don and his group to deliver the four-day team-building program. This sent a message to every hourly worker that this was, indeed, a new day.

The shared vision should result in all those involved modeling the behavior required by the vision. Don saw this illustrated one day when he was working the second shift as a cofacilitator. PICE was running four workshops that week on second shift for 20 people in each program. Over lunch break, the facilitators got together and said, "There was tremendous anxiety about the new body shop." Don asked, "What are the issues?" Richard, a lead facilitator, stated that everyone was concerned about the working environment. The facilitators thought that it would help the anxiety if they took each of the four coed classes into the new body shop, but they were discouraged from doing so by some of the GM managers.

Don paid more attention to the shared vision than the discouraging managers. He put on a hard hat and got hard hats and safety glasses for the members of the workshop that he was cofacilitating. Don arranged one-hour guided tours of the new body shop for the other three groups. The anxiety about the new body shop was outpaced by the tangible excitement you could feel throughout the entire learning center.

In one night, the facilitators demonstrated sound team behavior and a positive attitude in response to an issue. They diffused much of the anxiety and relieved the stress that many had felt. The actions they took said, in effect, "We will make this location the best plant in all of General Motors."

Of course, there were holdouts to the shared vision. Don immediately got called on the carpet by one of the GM managers who was trying to control the situation and hadn't bought into a leadership model that was about empowering people and truly building teams. But the shared vision prevailed; the good news was that the new plant manager at the Wilmington facility was from the Saturn Corporation. Its culture was based on the team concept. The new plant manager truly understood this critical moment in the overall history of the Wilmington plant and defended Don's actions.

The shared vision also required participation at all levels. The new plant manager appeared in every four-day program. This was quite a sacrifice; some days this involved being there from 6 AM to midnight. Many of the auto workers had never been in the same room at the same time with their plant manager. Modeling is a powerful device.

This story of PICE Inc. and the $8,000 contract that grew to over a half-million dollars comes back to the principles of understanding others and sharing the vision. Understanding the UAW and Saturn managers made all the difference. The motivation was strong, and the stakes high—the shutting down of the plant would end a half-century of production at the Wilmington facility (that had already been voted on and approved by the GM Board of Directors)—Wilmington got a reprieve: if the UAW would agree to the team concept, the plant would stay open. No one wanted to see the plant close and, at the same time, no one understood how to implement the team concept.

When PICE arrived on-site, you could cut the labor tension in the air with a knife. The transition to the team concept at the plant would prove to be painful and difficult. We involved management and labor in the design to make sure we got to the desired level of shared vision and values. The process of creating the shared vision led directly to the success of the team-building effort for Saturn.

STEADFAST RESOLVE TO SHARED VISION

Any entrepreneurs who want to grow and lead others must be steadfast in their resolve to adhere to the values of the organization and its shared vision. It's common to hear of companies who have lost their way, no longer have a "soul," or have "changed" in the eyes of consumers and employees. Those changes can almost always be traced back to a decaying of values and a skewing of the mission. That doesn't mean that a company's vision can't be tweaked, but, any time there is a major shift in values, vision, and mission, it often means a tough road ahead.

When it comes to getting to know your prospects and clients, it takes the skills to listen, the self-control to know when not to speak, and the knowledge to translate what is said into a meaningful foundation of what the person who said it really meant. To understand others, the leader knows that behind each statement told to him or her are a person's lifetime of values, behaviors, joys, triumphs, sorrows, and other layers of imprints, traits, and attributes that must be deciphered.

UNDERSTANDING YOUR EMPLOYEES

Although we've spent quite a bit of time on understanding others from a client perspective, there's a whole other side that will either create drive or dive in your venture. That, dear friends, is understanding your employees, subcontractors, and potential employees.

As an entrepreneur, you have certain attributes that have pushed you to where you are. These attributes lead you to strive for where you want to be. But there comes a moment when you will face the issue of your first hire. The first is the most important. It will set the pattern for the next 100.

It may seem easier to just hire anyone who walks through your door when you're in need of an employee. But trust us—that will do more harm than good most of the time. Hiring the "right" person is one of the most important things you will do. The right person will seize your vision and act on it. Hire for attitude first and skills second. An employee can always learn skills, but attitude is a different story. Hiring wrong is a disaster. Russell Simons stated our point of view when he said, "I've been blessed to find people who are smarter than I am, and they help me to execute the vision I have."

Find people who share your vision and values. They must comprehend your strategies and be willing to help you execute them. As you grow your business, you will undoubtedly run across very talented people who you think will fit well into your enterprise. Until you study and understand what makes a person tick, however, you won't really know. From that point of view, it makes sense to work at finding out as much as you can about the vision and values of the people who will represent your company before you hire them.

One of the strongest hires Don ever made was based on over three years of observations and experiences while working with Steve at another company. When Learning Resources needed a manager in 1984, Don made the decision to hire Steve, and it resulted in hiring just the right person at just the right time. Don and Steve shared the same vision and core values and saw the opportunity with GM through the same lens. That hiring decision put together the skills of the entrepreneurial visionary, strategist, and marketer with that of the financial manager and project manager. They became a leadership team. Together, they set about the task of hiring all the subcontractors, continuing the practice of working to find the right people as the project grew.

WHEN IT'S TIME TO LET AN EMPLOYEE GO

One of Dan's midwestern clients, Mel, owns a construction firm. His biggest problem is not getting bids, closing sales, or finding new leads. His problem is finding and hiring people who, as he says, "get it." He doesn't mean folks who will go to the convenience store to pick up lunch—he means people who understand his values and vision. There have been times when he has had Project Manager positions open for months on end; not because there aren't willing bodies walking into his establishment, but because they aren't the kind of people whom he feels understand his philosophy of business. He knows that hiring the wrong person is worse than not having anyone at all.

Another one of Dan's clients, Julie, asked him to work with her and her salespeople. Dan noticed that one of the members of her sales team was not performing well. During coaching sessions, Dan realized that the employee's philosophy about sales and life in general was far different from Julie's and the other members of the team. Although diversity of thought is a wonderful thing that can help companies grow, having an outlook that does not reflect the vision, key strategies, and values of the company and its owner can create a situation that at best leads to low productivity and at worst spreads to other people and parts of the organization and becomes a disruptive factor.

Without hesitation, Dan advised Julie to let her poor performer go. This action is a genuine service to the worker who is laid off. As they discussed the worker's dismissal, they realized that it was the best situation for him. Because he didn't fit in with the company's culture, he may find an enterprise that would make him happy and where he'd fit right in (philosophy and all). It took Julie three months to find another salesperson, but, when she did, it was a woman who had passed the vision, values, and philosophy tests. During her interviews, she was asked many situational sales questions that unveiled her thought processes as well as her outlook on life. In addition, they assessed her values, interests, behavior, and sales skills through computerized assessment vehicles.

Julie finally felt that she understood what the jobholder needed to be and that this woman was the individual to fulfill those needs. When she finally came on board, we knew that she "got it" and would perform quite well in her sales position. And, sure enough, she did!

Another client on the East Coast had a Director of Human Resources (HR) who was liked by everyone. He was a wonderful guy who was light-hearted, funny, and always on time to work. There was, however one glaring problem: He had a difficult time doing his job. The company had too many open jobs. Production was faltering, existing employees were overtaxed, and morale was getting worse.

Dan was not shy in telling his client that, unless he found a new Director of HR, his personnel problems would continue to get worse, perhaps even become insurmountable. Dan's suggestion was to get a new HR Director. The longer the existing one stayed, he told his client, the harder it would be to fill other vacant employee positions.

After much soul searching, the client finally saw the light. Even though he felt like he was firing his son, he knew that, for the good of the company, he was making the right move. Today, the company is fully staffed and production is at its peak. His new Director of HR went right to work contacting many of the organizations we mentioned in the last chapter, received a number of qualified candidates, and then took the extra step to make sure that they had more than the necessary skills to perform the job. They also had the mental and emotional perspectives that were in line with the company's values, strategies, and vision. The new Director mentioned to Dan many times how important it was for him to know that, though people may take a different route to reach the same goal, as long as they understood and saw life with the same overriding value system, worked in a manner consistent with those values as well as the vision and mission of the company, it was fine with him.

CREATING SHARED VISION AND VALUES WHILE EXPANDING THE COMPANY

One of Dan's experiences bears out the importance of understanding others to create shared vision and values. When For Eyes started to need more employees, it was extremely important to Dan that the individuals he hired understood his business philosophy. With one store, Dan could directly supervise each employee. However, opening new stores posed a problem: How could Dan ensure that this vision, mission, and values were understood and upheld in each location?

The solution Dan came up with was simple: He didn't let anyone manage a new location unless they first worked at the original store. This enabled Dan to size up each employee as to his or her business philosophy and basic outlook on life. Once he understood those all important elements in each person, and if that person jelled with what he saw as necessary to help his business flourish, that person was free to take on the position of store manager in another store.

It took about six months to assess the would-be manager's values, outlook, and general philosophy of life. During those six months, new managers would also learn the founding philosophy so that they could pass it on to others. This scenario was replicated many times over with people wanting to open stores in San Francisco, Los Angeles, Boston, and other cities. Each person spent six months in the original location. Without the fear of hiring people who would not understand the company's vision, mission, and values, Dan felt confident that each new area would thrive.

The same held true for Dan's management, marketing, advertising, and public relations firm. The company's culture was as important in that endeavor as it was at the optical company. People who worked there were understood to have the qualities necessary to fulfill and share the values and vision of Goldberg, Strunk, and Levy. That included having fun and laughing a lot. Because creativity is an important component of a marketing firm, people who feel comfortable and secure in that type of environment are more likely to be chosen for positions within the firm.

VIRTUAL BUSINESSES

Sharing vision and values in the virtual world and over large geographic areas in today's complex business environment can be very difficult. Don faced this issue at the SBDC, which was a government agency, housed by a university, and modeling online learning for entrepreneurial companies throughout the region. The question was how to build a shared vision and shared values with governmental agencies and for-profit companies while working in a university environment. The answer came back to listening—really listening—and understanding the problems of these very different entities; constantly executing key strategies by getting them to buy in; and taking time to figure out what would make them more effective.

Don had to make it a win-win situation for all parties. Intense, frequent communications became essential in creating shared vision and values. In addition to telephones, teleconferences, and email, virtual technologies like Webinars and online newsletters became very important.

LOOK FOR THE VISION AND MISSION IN VENDORS

The next time you're shopping for yourself, your family, or your business, take a few moments to look at the people who are selling to customers, servicing clients, or handling administrative functions within the establishments. Do they convey the vision and mission you would expect from the companies they work for? How does the answer, whether yes or no, make you feel? Although philosophies, values, and a company's mission are ideals and concepts, they can create a feeling that is pervasive throughout an enterprise.

When you walk into your local supermarket, clothing store, department store, professional office, or any other enterprise, try to think about what the founder envisioned when he or she started the company. If you get the feeling that the business has a "soul," gives you a good feeling, makes you want to come back, it's because the employees have relayed an energy to you that sent that message your way. Once the bond of understanding is made between an entrepreneur and his or her employees, that same bond is usually passed on to customers. It's a beautiful thing to see. When a shared vision and value system permeate a business, it can easily relate to lower turnover, higher productivity, and greater customer loyalty.

Not long ago, a local supermarket chain in our area was sold to a national company. Before the merger, the original owners touted their stores as family owned. We would see them strolling through the aisles on a frequent basis. They would address their employees on a first-name basis. The pride everyone had in the company was highly evident and consistent. No matter which store we'd go into, employees were relaxed, helpful, and smiling. Everyone knew the vision, mission, and values of the company and its owners; in fact, they were posted in the store for everyone to see.

Shortly after the merger went through, everything changed. The help seemed tense, laughter was more out of nervousness than fun, employees informed us that they were told that "mystery shoppers" would be sent in from the new company's main office to assess things. Dialogue with customers seemed scripted (which it was), and the lightness that had been the hallmark of the company had evaporated. It seemed like the new owners hadn't realized that what made the old company successful was that everyone understood and shared the vision, mission, and values of the original owners. If they had only let that foundation stay in place and even built upon it and reinforced it, they wouldn't have seen sales decline between 17% and 20% at most locations.

These stories all exemplify how important it is to understand others and create the shared vision. The question comes back to you. How do you want your entrepreneurial venture to be viewed?

KEY POINTS AND LESSONS LEARNED

- ☑ Sharing your vision and values allows you to connect with those who hold the same or similar values. Sharing forms the basis of loyalty and efficient use of resources.
- ☑ People buy based on emotion.
- ☑ Empathy is the best way to start a relationship.
- ☑ Listening skills; hear opportunities crying for help.
- ☑ Hire the right person based on attitude; he or she can learn skills.
- ☑ Hire people who embrace the company's vision and share its values.
- ☑ Effective leaders model the behaviors they want their employees to have.

7

Empowerment and Expansion of Your Employees and Your Business

Taking your company to the next level involves empowering yourself as well as those who work for and with you. Through empowerment, your team will experience greater creativity and a free flow of ideas to help drive you toward your vision. Entrepreneurs who try to do everything themselves may quickly realize that they've become hemmed into a situation of stagnation. The effective entrepreneurial leader allows employees to establish themselves in positions of responsibility, make mistakes, learn, and grow. In this chapter, we will start by posing eight questions. Then we will walk you through several examples on how to empower and grow while remaining true to your vision and mission.

In a previous chapter, Dan discussed how he expanded For Eyes by enabling employees to run offices in new markets. However, before they could travel to their desired locations, he insisted that they work directly with him for six months. This experience enabled Dan and the would-be district manager to get to know each other. It also helped Dan to decide whether or not each employee grasped the philosophy that was the foundation of the organization. After he saw that the new manager deeply understood that caring for people was more important than chasing the last dollar of profit, Dan was happy to turn responsibility over to the folks who would expand his business and philosophy.

It is impossible to grow a business without the extra efforts of people outside of the founding entrepreneur. There is only so much capacity that one person can produce. Time, energy, and other resources that each individual has are finite. To expand, the effective entrepreneurial leader must build two teams: an external team (discussed in previous chapters as the Success Team) to help plan the expansion, and an internal team of employees to make the expansion happen. Let's turn our attention to how to build an employee team.

Figure 7.1
Leadership Model—Empowerment and Expansion of Your Employees and
Your Business

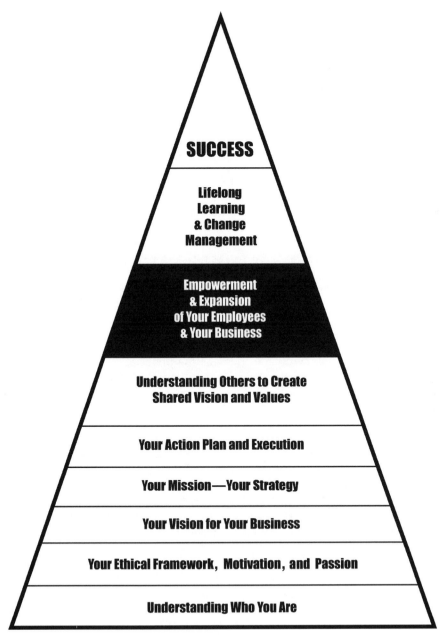

EMPLOYEE TEAM QUESTIONS

Here are eight questions to answer as you form your first employee team:

- Do you have a clear understanding of the skills you need from the team members?
- Do you have a time frame in which to hire and train the team members?
- Do you have a definite role and responsibility for each team member?
- Do you have a plan of how you will integrate new employees into the team?
- Do you have an ideal number of people in mind for your first team?
- Do you have an idea of the time it will take you to bring the entire team up-to-speed?
- Have you thought through how this team will change your role as the leader?
- Who will be your first hire and why should they come first?

AN EXAMPLE OF THE PROCESS OF EMPOWERMENT

When Don started Learning Resources, he spent four months answering the eight questions. First, he devoted a lot of time to finding the core group of team members who had the skills needed to run the project for General Motors in the short term and over the long haul. Don was the sales and marketing strategist and knew he needed someone else to manage the operations of the learning center and manage the financial side of the business. Finding the "right" first team member was a critical moment in the life of this startup. After making the decision to bring Steve on as a partner in the enterprise, Don and Steve set about the task of designing a plan to hire and train their learning center staff.

They realized that to successfully manage a two-shift and ultimately a three-shift operation for six days a week, they needed a plan with a specific timeline. Don remembers Steve asking, "How are we going to figure out the center's operation if we start with two shifts immediately?" As the leader, Don listened to Steve, and rethought the path ahead. They reduced the scope of the project to ensure a high-quality operation because quality was the cornerstone of the vision and mission.

They decided to start with a pilot program running on the first shift. They picked a first-shift "A-Team." They empowered the A-Team and prepared them for the growth they saw on the horizon. Then, they were ready to hire and phase in the second-shift operation in the GM learning center. They utilized the skills and knowledge of the A-Team to "train the trainers" on the second shift. This process smoothed out any problems in the operation, and they were able to integrate everyone into the team successfully. The process also allowed them to demonstrate their quality vision and mission and, most important, their passion for the project to all their hires. Every team member knew and felt that their ideas and suggestions would be taken seriously. They also celebrated each milestone that they achieved together as a team.

The way Don and Steve ramped up the project gave the GM managers and the UAW trainers a clear sense that they had hired the right company for the job. Eventually the behavior of employee empowerment they modeled would be integrated into the culture of all the GM skill trades. The way the pilot was implemented showed GM managers that the "new way" worked.

RIGHT ATTITUDE LEADERSHIP

It is up to the leaders of a company to promote positive attitudes. A number of years ago, Dan spoke to a large group of people who worked for a concrete manufacturing company. Prior to his speaking engagement, he had the opportunity to sit with one of the two founders over lunch at a country club so he could get a clear understanding of the philosophy of the company, its mission and vision, how executives and other employees interact, and any other key points or problems that should be addressed before he spoke. What the founder revealed was insightful. He mentioned that he and his partner started the company decades ago, and since then they had never wavered from one major tenet: Right Attitude Leadership. Dan recognized the evidence of that statement by the lapel pin worn by his luncheon partner. It simply said "Attitude." After further questioning, the founder replied that Right Attitude Leadership means teamwork and commitment to customers and employees. He said that too many companies concentrate on their customers without realizing that, if their employees are unhappy, their customers will likely become dissatisfied in the long run.

Paying attention to employees makes perfect sense. Having employees with the right attitude will have a direct and immediate positive impact on customers. Dissatisfied employees eventually will pass their feelings on to others by their actions, words, or lack of initiative. Sour employees will mean sour customer service, low retention rates of clients and staff, and a stifled growth process.

GROWING YOUR EMPLOYEES

Giving employees the power to grow, take responsibility, and build camaraderie will pay off in high morale, low turnover, greater revenues, and expansion. Ask any entrepreneur what her greatest asset is and she'll probably tell you her people. During the general citywide elections in the mid-1980s, Dan's marketing company was hired to help the campaign of an individual running for a major elected office in Philadelphia. Although Dan knew all the parties involved in the situation, his partner, Dave, had a better grasp of the town's media as well as longer relationships with the city's electronic and print journalists. Empowerment in this situation meant giving Dave the lead responsibility on this project.

The question became: how do you make a client comfortable with an individual you know has the capability to do an excellent job when he looks toward you to be the person in control? This issue is a recurring situation for most growing entrepreneurs and their companies. Dan solved it by setting up a meeting, having all the major players sit and discuss strategy, who would handle what, and how things would get implemented. After introducing his colleague and giving some of his biographical information, Dan told the assembled group that, though he would oversee the campaign, the go-to person would be his partner, Dave. Dave would be the one to appear at rallies, interact with the press, and be responsible for positioning the candidate. Dan emphasized that he had complete confidence in Dave's ability.

As the leader, you are the face of the business and clients always want you. This limits your enterprise's growth. You must begin, as Dan did in this case, and explain to the customer that the right person for this job is Dave. Also, you must communicate that you will support and back up Dave's decisions. Dave was ready to grow, and as a leader it is your job to guide people to the next level. Theodore Roosevelt said, "The best executive is the one who has sense enough to pick good men to do what he wants done, and self-restraint enough to keep from meddling with them while they do it."

As November rolled around, the momentum increased for our previously unknown candidate. The candidate appeared frequently on the major local television networks, on the appropriate radio stations, and in the most important newspapers and magazines. Election Day proved him to be the winner. Dave was ecstatic, as was the candidate, who held the position for four straight four-year terms. Dan learned that by giving people the opportunity to prove themselves, employees will rise to the occasion. But you have to let them.

During the course of that year, other employees of the marketing firm were given the ability to handle their own clients while Dan stuck to his strategy of enabling people to grow by empowering them. The more he empowered others, the more he could do what he felt he should be doing—getting more business.

This theme repeats itself in every venture. More people leave companies because they've been repressed than because they're not making enough money. Entrepreneurs who allow their folks to blossom will soon find out that the same thing happens to their business. One of the most exciting experiences you can have as a business owner is seeing that look in the eye of your employee and the looks from the rest of the team that says, "We did good!"

By the same token, leaders must keep an eye on their subordinates to make sure that they're following the process they've put in place. Even people who have been taken through the stages of understanding the philosophy of the company and its founders can stray. It's common for people to misunderstand power and think it means "controlling" others.

Real power means letting people grow while the leader guides them toward a goal. Real entrepreneurial leaders find and empower good people.

Blaine Lee sums this up with the metaphor of great orchestral music: "The great leaders are like the best conductors—they reach beyond the notes to reach the magic in the players."

LEADERSHIP: DEALING WITH A PROBLEM MANAGER

About five years ago, Dan was facilitating a weeklong management seminar for a trash-to-fuel company. The founders of the organization were typical entrepreneurs: they had a vision; formulated a mission and accompanying strategy; worked hard to put together the financing, staff, and facilities; went out and got clients; and turned over the day-to-day operations of the plants to others. However, one of the company's major facilities was run by an excessive micromanager who was known for what employees called "turn over the bucket management."

Dan was curious to find out what that meant and posed the question to the twenty-three managers in attendance. Their response was revealing. The micromanager (we'll call him Jim), would oversee every task minutely. If a problem occurred at work, Jim would call anyone he felt could help alleviate the situation. Then he would turn over a bucket, sit on it, and watch them work. He would do this even if the problem happened after normal hours and he had to call people back into the plant. His staff had become accustomed to his behavior. They expected him to oversee any and all functions personally. This became overwhelming; people felt none of them was capable of doing their jobs completely on their own. His micromanagement was stunting employee growth.

This is an extreme case, but it demonstrates that it can happen even to the most trusting entrepreneurial leader. To avoid the problem, keep your eyes and ears open to situations that may cause employee unrest or create demotivating behavior. Anything that leads to slippage in productivity should be a concern to anyone who empowers their employees. It's always good to check in with your employees. Once in a while, arrange an unscheduled lunch to say "thanks" and ask a few questions. You should ask open-ended questions such as, "What are some concerns the team has with the current project?" Listen and take mental notes. Ask more questions and dig deeper and really listen. Then get "permission" to take a few notes so together the team can build an action plan to deal with some critical problems.

Incidentally, never discuss people's performance in a negative way in a group setting. You are the leader, and you will take action based on what you have heard at lunch. All effective leaders must make sure to delegate without micromanaging, while knowing what your employees are doing to carry out their tasks. It is a balancing act that must be perfected.

You may be wondering how the above scenario was resolved. Jim was fired and replaced by Bob. Bob was an empowering manager, the kind every entrepreneurial leader should strive to hire. His first statements to his managers on the initial day of the weeklong training session were, "Do you folks want to have a life? Do you want to do your jobs the way you always felt you should? Do you want to go home at a normal hour? Then, let's start by changing the culture."

Interestingly enough, this was a difficult transition. Because most employees were watched over so closely, Jim was, in fact, almost doing their jobs for them. Some employees weren't sure how to make the change. Slowly they began to see that, if they were empowered to really do their jobs on their own, they would advance.

The big shift became apparent the week Dan and Bob were cloistered with all the managers in the conference room for training. Staff were told that unless it was a family emergency or a problem that involved a nuclear component at the plant, the managers were not to be disturbed. An amazing thing happened. On the Wednesday of the training week, there was a breakdown of one of the four boilers in the plant. That meant that 25% of the plant's output was in danger. Because none of the managers' crews was allowed to inform them, the staff members had to figure out how to take care of the problem on their own. Without management's input, the crew members went to work and fixed the problem, and the plant had its highest output day on record. Needless to say, at the end of the day's seminar when the managers were told about what happened, they were quite proud of their crews. It was this event that brought home the realization that if you empower your employees, they can do incredible things.

The era of long days and always fighting fires was over. Each person began to buy into the new culture, in which each person took responsibility for his or her job. You could feel the energy, see the enthusiasm, and hear the excitement; it was a turning point in the plant. Productivity rose, and management and staff had a new confidence that had been absent up to that point.

LEADERSHIP: EXAMPLES OF EMPOWERMENT AND GROWTH

If you've ever been on the receiving end of someone who tried to control your actions, you can comprehend how it lowers your desire to perform, creates undue angst, and leaves you demotivated. That's why it's not surprising that the companies who often have the highest earnings are the ones listed in the category, "Best places to work."

The 3M Company has long been recognized for empowering their employees to create the next generation of 3M products. Post-it Notes is a great story of employee empowerment. From Spencer Silver's efforts to develop a strong adhesive came Arthur Fry's realization that the weak adhesive Spencer had actually developed helped to keep his papers in place without damaging his choir book. Clearly the ability of an employee to experiment and suggest products and services made those little brightly colored squares one of the world's most popular office products.

Enabling employees to express themselves without fear of retribution, ridicule, or being laughed at can help businesses grow. When a culture of nonjudgmental listening is promoted, people feel that whatever they have to say or contribute will be handled with respect. This feeling often develops into a creative culture within your company.

Don had that experience when several of his management teams in the landscaping business wanted to reorganize the business. By listening to their concerns and their proposal, Don was able to suggest creating new teams based upon the key functional areas. The company was divided into a "tree business," a "shrub care business," a "deck construction business," and a "lawn maintenance business." It took a while, but this division proved to be the right way to empower employees and grow the business.

AVENUES OF LEARNING

As you lay out expansion plans, you will realize that, without having the right employees on board, it will be very difficult to achieve your goals. Once you have the people in place to make your move, it's time to think about where you want your enterprise to go. This is why having the vision statement, writing down the key strategies, and knowing your mission is critical at this point. You are about to grow your business—a very exciting time in every owner's life. In Figure 7.2, you can see that you must create "Avenues of Learning" to help empower your employees while expanding your business. The key is to build the "Avenues of Learning" that you will need for all your new people as the business grows.

Avenues of Learning are based on adult Learning theory. In short, you are not creating a typical school-like educational program. You are creating learning opportunities that are beneficial to the learner and match their behavior in the work environment.

Learning is best at the experiential level. You experience it: you touch it, feel it, smell it, hear it. You make an emotional connection to it. You own it! You hired people for their positive attitude, and by providing avenues of learning you let them know how much you want them to grow and prosper in the business. That is a powerful message that people can understand. Learning will become an everyday thing not a once-in-a-while occurrence.

EXPANDING YOUR BUSINESS

Let's share some thoughts about the role the Internet will play, the importance of market research, the use of your A-Team and capital.

If you are considering expanding your product line, think about what you're currently selling and what additional products would complement your inventory. For instance, if televisions and electronic equipment make up your business, we don't think you should start hawking underwear! But things that go with watching TV that most people don't consider, like serving bowls, glassware, and other food-related items that many folks use

Figure 7.2
The Period of Transition

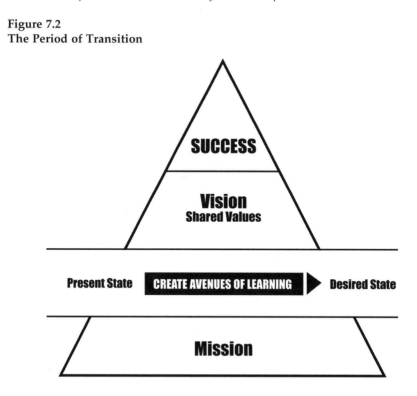

when viewing their favorite shows or DVDs, might set you apart. After all, what do you see when you look at commercials for televisions: people watching a baseball, football, basketball, or hockey game while eating some sort of snack and drinking some type of beverage. Some officially licensed major sports league products might be a natural fit. You might consider anything that people might use when watching TV. Let your mind go a bit and recruit your empowered employees to do the same.

Consider additional products or services that might work with the Internet. With the trend of higher energy costs today, every company should look at the Internet as a part of their strategy. One example is keeping your customers informed about the current status of products and services.

The Internet can help you expand your market by reaching more people without the high cost of mailing out newsletters. To do a newsletter and send it postal mail is at least two dollars per copy. To do a high-end, electronic newsletter with lots of color and graphics, the cost is dimes not dollars. You can send electronic newsletters more times per year than an expensive mailer (though be careful not to send too often or your potential customers will consider your emails spam). In any case, the Web must be part of your expansion plans.

Creative, free-flowing thought is one of the best ways to expand your business, but keep your product and/or service in line with the demographics of your market. There is no substitute for good market research. Customer surveys are an easy way to gain some insights. You should survey your customers and ask at least three questions:

1. Did you like your experience with our company?
2. Would you recommend our products or services to others?
3. What other services might we offer you in the future that you would be interested in?

If you own a bricks-and-mortar business and you want to add another location, think about what is making your existing store or office successful. It is common to hear about companies that expand so fast that they grow themselves out of existence. The desire to expand must be tempered with the reality that accompanies it. When you take the time to analyze your expansion plan, the first thing you must address is market research. Next, ask if you have the staff and capital to make the new location successful.

Assuming that all the people you have are in lock step with your philosophy, there's the other situation of numbers. Sometimes, the entrepreneur becomes obsessed with the thought of expansion, and even though they believe that they can find the right people to run the new location, they often put the proverbial cart before the horse—they sign a lease and are stuck with trying to find employees. A better approach may be to scout the new locale for potential help, get in touch with the employment resources we outlined in Chapter 6, interview prospective employees, get a feel for the area, and do research, more research, and even more research. Think through all your financial projections for the new location. Then, consider what will happen if sales come slower than you forecasted. What if costs are higher than you forecasted? Think research.

EMPLOY THE A-TEAM

If you're lucky enough to have identified the necessary employees, found a good location, and put your marketing plan in place, be careful of hiring new folks to run the shop without the direct and in-person supervision of someone from the "main office." Consider the "A-Team" approach. The A-Team knows the mission and the strategies. They can help to instill an understanding of the vision and how every employee is connected to that dream on a deadline. Muster your A-Team's "strike force" to set up new offices and get them running like a top while reinforcing the training the new staff receives. Use the A-Team to help you to build the necessary "Avenues of Learning." If you are fortunate enough to have a superb "strike force," you can almost expand at will (providing you've done the proper research and have the necessary capital).

Ah yes, capital. Expansion can suck up capital faster than a Hoover set on high. We have seen many companies whose cash flow providers (products, services, and/or locations) get drained by keeping the expansion entities afloat. Cash flow is king in business today. Having good cash flow and cash in the bank are essential prerequisites to expanding. It's always better to expand slowly. Allocate your resources realistically, giving a set time frame for the expansion vehicle to turn the corner. If it doesn't, be prepared to say, "Hey, that didn't work, close it up." If you decide to let your new idea die, there may be ways to revive it at another place or time. Market conditions change, and you just may have been ahead of (hopefully not behind) the times.

EXPANDING FOR EYES

Dan's goal was to expand For Eyes to encircle the Delaware Valley (the greater Philadelphia area), and the Lehigh Valley (its cousin to the north in Pennsylvania that includes Allentown, Bethlehem, and Easton). Enamored with the thought of doing for the Allentown area what he did for the Philadelphia area, he set out to do a minicoup in one fell swoop. Dan thought: "Why not open a shop in Allentown and Easton at the same time and have locations at both ends of the Valley?" Not a bad idea at the outset. A problem soon emerged: finding a viable store location in downtown Easton proved difficult, much more difficult than Allentown. Nonetheless, Dan opened both stores anyway. Allentown did quite well, the public relations kicked in, and business at the store was soon jumping. Easton, on the other hand, languished. Even an article in the *Easton Express*, the local daily newspaper, didn't seem to help. The truth was, Easton had yet to go through its "revival" and was not yet ready for the business. Lesson learned: It would have been better for Dan to understand the environment he was entering at a local and regional level before he spent the money to expand.

Although Easton wasn't making money, it really wasn't losing much either. A time frame was set for what would be closure or profitability. Entrepreneurial leaders cannot let their ego get in the way of success. The date came and, though it was tough to close the Easton location, there was no other choice. For Eyes was ready to expand into the South, so it made sense to "move" the Easton location to Richmond, Virginia. That proved to work out quite well; it turned a profit almost from day one.

Even the best-laid plans can go awry. Entrepreneurial leaders are willing to accept the results and continue to forge ahead. They measure the results against benchmarks they set up and then take action on the results. It's during the situations that don't work out that others will look to see the reaction of the leader.

Don used benchmarks and measurements to make a major decision regarding his landscaping company. In year three they withdrew from servicing residential accounts. Originally, his team had thought that the residential accounts were the foundation of the company, but the numbers told a different story. Residential clients had become the least profitable part of the business.

Of course, it was not just a command decision. In keeping with leadership principles, Don involved all the managers and employees in this decision, and they were a stronger company for doing it that way. Leaders know that it's those trials and tribulations that will test their strength. The successful leader will carry his or her enterprise forward by keeping employees focused and on board with the choices that must be made. The way he or she handles adversity will either gain added respect or create negativity.

THE EXPANSION OF A SOFTWARE BUSINESS

The vast majority of businesses today are in the service sector. Service industries can run into situations that either spawn plague or prosperity. A client of ours owns a software company. It has a sizable staff with a responsive customer service team. The programmers developed a software package that helped their target audience substantially. The young entrepreneurial owners put together a plan that set thresholds to know when to hire additional employees. As soon as they saw sales approaching the first threshold, they would begin interviewing for additional help. Their timing was extraordinary. As each revenue mark was hit, they would bring new staff members on board. The plan included time for training before it was necessary to integrate the new individuals into the business flow. Like clockwork, our clients built a force that enabled their company to grow, their customers to feel appreciated and receive superb service, and their sales team to add even more customers.

The more they grew, the more they showed their employees how much they enjoyed having them in the company. Once a week, sessions were held in which everyone within the organization was free to express their thoughts about anything without fear of retribution. It was during one of those meetings that an employee came up with an idea for a feature that would add a whole new dimension to the software program. By implementing the new feature, sales rose even more aggressively. The bonus received by the individual who came up with the idea spurred others to think even more creatively. The cycle of continued growth that our client has experienced has been amazing and has not yet stopped.

Planning for growth should include best/worst scenarios. Going back to the software company, the owners had initially projected sales that many thought were much too optimistic. Although they had conservative and midrange projections as well, their personal intuitions led them to believe that the higher revenue numbers were most accurate—and indeed, that turned out to be the case.

All the scenarios should be based on sound research, customer surveys, and feedback from the entire team. When your team buys in and sees this as helping the company reach your vision, extraordinary things happen. If you have a ceiling as well as a floor, you can prepare for situations that others may see as insurmountable.

Another client of ours relies on workers who come to the United States on H2B visas—visas for well-educated and highly skilled guest workers. Congress controls the number of people who can enter the country through the H2B program. Recognizing the possibility that the downsizing of H2B might occur and would affect sales, the company planned out a few alternatives, using ingenuity to stave off problems.

The hope would be that the H2B workers would indeed be able to enter the country, and the company would have all the labor they needed. However, another alternative involved slowing growth by not taking on any new clients but retaining the ones they already had. The third alternative incorporated bonuses to any current employee who referred a potential employee who was later hired. The company might also add a recruiter and use some of the recruiting resources mentioned earlier.

As the company monitored the H2B legislation debate, the management team would discuss the implementation of alternatives. Once it became increasing clear that its regular labor force might not be appearing from south of the border, they had to decide between alternative number 2 and number 3. Because the sales team had been receiving requests from potentially new clients, and other opportunities were becoming evident, alternative number 3 was the only realistic choice. Having a plan made it much easier to begin the process of finding new employees. Because the company didn't wait until the final decision from Washington, D.C., they had a jump start on their competition. Employees, knowing that they stood to gain monetarily, began referring folks to add to the labor pool. Having built and created some strategic partners had real benefits in this situation. The recruiter went out to all the resources available to find additional help, and others within the company stepped up to volunteer to work extra hours if necessary (that's called loyalty). Training classes were started as scheduled within alternative 3, and, by the time the workers were needed on the front lines, everyone was ready.

Were there glitches? Sure. But our client showed leadership during the ordeal, and, because everyone noticed the resolve that was shown, it was very difficult for the staff not to join the cause wholeheartedly. As it turned out, the organization experienced significant growth, and it used the methods it had established through alternative 3 to expand into two new geographic areas.

By empowering your employees, you stand to make growth a simpler process. When your team understands your action plan, how you intend to execute it, and it witnesses your energy to follow it through with the help of a fully engaged staff, the entrepreneurial leader can do magical things.

Expansion can become a smooth process, even when it doesn't work out exactly as planned. Effective leaders can respond and react with a clear understanding of the consequences of their actions. They can build a team around them that can charge into the business world with insight, fun, knowledge, and empowerment. That's when it becomes easier to overcome obstacles and/or build to the next level.

KEY POINTS AND LESSONS LEARNED

- ☑ Empowering employees leads to higher levels of creativity, involvement, and productivity.
- ☑ Effective leaders model the behavior they want from their employees.
- ☑ Sour employees mean sour customer service and bitter feelings.
- ☑ Don't micromanage.
- ☑ Challenge employees through delegation to grow into decision makers.
- ☑ Create "Avenues of Learning" to empower your employees.
- ☑ Leaders think about what they could do to offset negative factors before they happen.

8

Lifelong Learning and Change Management

We have discussed the realm of entrepreneurial leadership throughout the pages of this book, but, in the end, individual growth is the underpinning of it all. As any successful entrepreneur knows, continuous learning is the fuel that enables new ideas to flourish, curiosity to turn into profits, and energy to transition into viable enterprises. There is an old Chinese proverb that says, "Learning is a treasure that will follow its owner everywhere."

We will explore two models in this chapter. One is a lifelong learning model and the other is a proven sales process for your business. These two models will help you to sustain growth and adapt to the ever-changing world of business.

Let's talk about the fuel that will lead you to growth and more profits. Many business writers and entrepreneurs suggest that creating a learning culture in business is no longer a nice thing to do; rather, it is a necessity. To start, let us pose some questions to you as the leader of your enterprise:

- How do you go about learning something new?
- Have you set aside time for learning?
- What do you like to read?
- What role does the Internet play in your daily life?
- How do you utilize TV to help you gain business insights?
- How do you get your financial/business news of the day?
- Who is available to coach you in the learning process?
- Do you attend Chamber of Commerce, Community College, SCORE, or SBDC learning events?
- Do you have a plan of how you will integrate new learning into your company?

Complacency and stagnation can create a death grip on a once-thriving business. Failing to listen to your customers and advisors, observe the market, watch your competitors, or stay abreast of the latest trends and techniques can cause your endeavor to disintegrate quickly. The entrepreneurial landscape is littered with companies that didn't keep up with the times or that were left behind the learning curve. From music to typewriters,

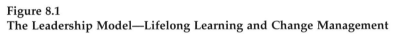
Figure 8.1
The Leadership Model—Lifelong Learning and Change Management

SUCCESS

Lifelong Learning & Change Management

Empowerment & Expansion of Your Employees & Your Business

Understanding Others to Create Shared Vision and Values

Your Action Plan and Execution

Your Mission—Your Strategy

Your Vision for Your Business

Your Ethical Framework, Motivation, and Passion

Understanding Who You Are

Figure 8.2
The Entrepreneur's Learning Model

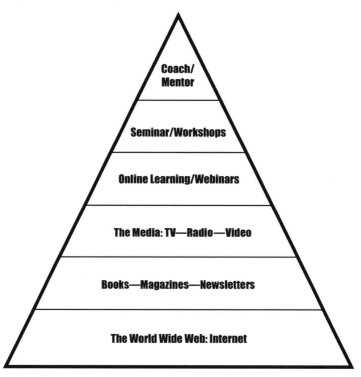

Coach/
Mentor

Seminar/Workshops

Online Learning/Webinars

The Media: TV—Radio—Video

Books—Magazines—Newsletters

The World Wide Web: Internet

mimeos to payphones, the stories within many industries relate tales of people who fought the future or failed to recognize an opportunity that was staring them in the face.

THE ENTREPRENEURIAL LEARNING MODEL

"All of the top achievers I know are life-long learners–looking for new skills, insights, and ideas. If they're not learning, they're not growing–not moving toward excellence." Denis Waitley, American motivational speaker and author of self-help books.

Most entrepreneurs are utilizing many resources in their daily quest for information. We've delineated six levels and have called it our "Entrepreneurial Learning Model." This learning model includes Web pages on the Internet, print materials such as books and magazines, media such as radio and TV, tutorials and Webinars, seminars and workshops, as well as live coaching and mentoring.

World Wide Web

We are living in revolutionary times because of Internet technology. As you look at the financial records of your company you will note that costs in most categories are rising. But there is one exception: the Internet. With the Internet we have the ability to communicate and market to our customers while managing our business at lower costs than traditional methods. The World Wide Web offers the promise of building interconnected communities of users that share the same interests.

The biggest issue with the Internet is that it requires change. Change is inevitable; in fact, it's the one thing in life that's constant. The effective leader knows that and prepares for it on an ongoing basis. Market demographics shift, consumer preferences and trends evolve, business-to-business demands ebb and flow. Without the ability to monitor your target group, you run the risk of falling out of the business race. The Internet provides entrepreneurs with fantastic resources to capture current and future customer buying patterns. Sites that provide marketing research information like www.forrester.com and www.claritas.com are tremendous resources for business leaders who are looking to grow.

The Internet is a portal to today's world of knowledge and information. Leaders benefit by learning how to interface with this powerful tool. Failure to learn how to use these resources can lead to falling behind competitors and wasting time. After all, time is an entrepreneurial leader's most valuable asset.

Books, Magazines, and Newsletters

Prior to the Internet, print media was how we got our business information. There is still a key role for print information sources. Reading business books can help entrepreneurs build their brand by keeping their minds open to what is happening now and what is forecast for the future. Most of us in business still depend on industry-specific magazines and newsletters to keep us current with the trends in our business. We find it insightful to read a biography of a prominent leader to gain new views of leadership thinking.

More and more today, print resources are accessible over the Internet. E-newsletters have become a cost-effective way to reach customers on a regular basis. Don faced a problem when he joined the Kutztown University SBDC—how could he reach more small businesses on a monthly basis? The print newsletter was expensive. The solution was an e-newsletter that has grown from an initial 600 subscribers in 2003 to over 8,000 in just four years. The cost is getting less and less even as we send more. That is representative of the knowledge revolution.

The Media: TV, Radio, and Video

Most business leaders were born and raised in the TV and radio era of the last 50 years. Television and radio allow entrepreneurs to view the world from a grander scale. Having a receptive view enables new and creative thoughts to enter your business mind. It's amazing how many businesspeople come up with their next great idea by watching TV or listening to the radio. Often these media enable an entrepreneur to recognize a niche that hasn't been filled. One strategy for learning is to take advantage of each of these information sources on a regular basis, tap into business shows on television, and rent or purchase business training videos.

Media has been transformed in the last decade because of the influence of the Internet and the associated technologies. Online videos are viewed by hundreds of millions of people, and yet this technology is less than a decade old. Recently, we have seen the advent of the podcast as a way of communicating the news. There are a number of subscription podcasts that you can listen to right on your desktop or on your iPod in the car.

Online Tutorials and Live Webinars

Some new technologies constitute a cost-effective solution for the entrepreneur to gain knowledge and experience in key business-related topics. There is an explosion in the development of online tutorials and modules—many of which have no charge or only a very minimal fee. Online modules provide self-paced, individualized learning twenty-four hours a day, seven days a week.

Most online learning modules run in length from 30 minutes to several hours. High-end Web-based learning modules will have streaming video and voiceovers that improve the learning experience. Online modules are advantageous because you don't have to leave your place of work to travel to a workshop or conference. As energy costs continue to climb, the trend may move even more strongly toward online learning.

Many of these courses are suitable to share with your team in a conference room setting using a projector. The Small Business Administration offers a large library of free online courses at www.sba.gov. You can find an even larger library of free courses at Kutztown Small Business Development Center at www.kutztownsbdc.org.

Webinars are the next learning technology to emerge in this decade, and they are just beginning to be utilized on a large scale. Rather than just a program that is run on the computer like a learning module, a Webinar is a live seminar that is conducted by a person across the Internet. All you need to participate is access to a telephone and a computer connected to the Internet over a broadband connection (a dial-up connection is too slow for a Webinar).

The most effective Webinars have a lot of interactivity between the host and the participants. Webinars allow the learner to "share the desktop" of the host. This enables you to work together, for example, to build out a cash flow statement in real time. Most Webinars have an audio or video capability as well (though calling into a teleconference is usually preferred for high-quality audio).

Seminars and Workshops

Live training is a more traditional approach to learning. The seminar or workshop adds the added dimension of being "away" from the office as well as the opportunity to network face-to-face. Throughout the United States, the entrepreneur is offered live workshops and seminars in their local area by community colleges, SCORE chapters, local SBDCs, and Chambers of Commerce. In addition, the entrepreneur can go to regional or national conferences in their industry.

Conferences offer two venues for learning. One is to attend scheduled workshops and the other is to visit vendor exhibits. Spending time in the exhibit hall talking to sales reps can provide you with invaluable information about trends in your business. Many businesspeople avoid those contacts like the proverbial plague because they don't want to be "sold to," but we are saying you can use the opportunity to make contacts with people who can help you learn more about what you need to know. First, identify, in a short list, what kind of information you want to obtain. Second, stay focused on your list and listen to the various vendor sales pitches. Salespeople, if they are good, will know the pulse and trends of your industry's businesses. Your objective is to get your handle on that information.

Coaches and Mentors

Once the exclusive tool of wealthy executives, coaches and mentors are more often becoming the key component of every entrepreneurial leader's learning program. "A single conversation with a wise man is better than ten years of study." Chinese Proverb. It is worth it to invest time and money to get coaching and mentoring from someone you respect. That person can help to guide you as you lead your enterprise.

Business coaching has come into its own for several reasons—the speed of change, the explosion of technology, the flattening of the globe, and the stress that leaders are under. All entrepreneurs, whether running a small proprietorship or a midsized corporation, need to find and nurture a relationship with someone who can help them guide their enterprise.

A lifelong learning model is critical to your ongoing business success. Learning will unlock the door to change with less pain. In Appendix A, we have provided a detailed list of books, magazines, and Websites that will get you started on the path to learning. You need to build a plan for yourself and stick to it. As Alvin Toffler said, "The illiterate of the 21st century will not be those who cannot read and write, but those who cannot learn, unlearn, and relearn."

LIFELONG LEARNING: THE SKILL OF SALES

The entrepreneurial leaders of growing organizations know that the responsibility for sales falls on their shoulders. Without sales there will be no business; it's tough to lead an organization when sales aren't coming in.

At the end of the day, selling yourself, your product, or your service is what it is all about.

All business leaders need to understand the selling process and be ready to support it. Dan and Don are known as "rainmakers." They make things happen by building relationships and, when the time is right, delivering their pitch.

While running Learning Resources on-site at GM, Don made a decision to send all of his staff and subcontractors to a four-day workshop on selling. At the time, Steve (his partner) asked, "Why are we doing this and what about the cost?" Don's response was, "Sales training will help build our team, and we will get a tenfold return on the investment." Having your entire team trained in selling gets everyone on the same page about being customer centric.

As the leader, you are the number-one salesperson in your company; that fact doesn't change as you grow the business. Even if you succeed at building a sizable sales team, you inevitably will be called upon to close a sale or forge a new sales horizon. You will be called upon by your employees in critical situations to help build relationships that will lead to major sales.

Selling is a game, and you have to decide whether or not you want to play. More important, do you have what it takes to win?

Procuring sales is not easy for most folks. The salesperson always seems to be at a disadvantage. Inexperienced salespeople automatically "sell to" the buyer rather than letting the buyer "buy from" them. People don't like to be sold, but they do like to buy. People have their own agenda; they are NOT going to buy just because you want them to. The more you force, the more they will push you away. It may seem counterintuitive, but the first thing an entrepreneur must learn to do is to "stop selling." No, that doesn't mean to close up shop and go home; "stop selling" means to take a different sales approach.

Dan developed a course over thirty-five years ago called The Six Steps to Solid Sales Success™ (Solid Sales) to help entrepreneurs, salespeople, and business leaders understand the selling process. Solid Sales explains how to maximize prospect and client lists, referral opportunities, closing rates, and revenues as well as how to increase effectiveness in reaching company goals.

Dan initially formulated these six steps and taught them to his retail and wholesale sales forces. These steps helped him build a very successful business. They can do the same for you.

THE SIX STEPS OF SOLID SALES SUCCESS™

Those Six Steps are:

1. Understanding who you are
2. Understanding others

3. Getting prospects
4. Making agreements
5. Adding value
6. Closing

Figure 8.3
The Six Steps to Solid Sales Success™

Closing

Adding Value

Making Agreements

Getting Prospects

Understanding Others

Understanding Who You Are

Understanding Who You Are

The first step of the sales process is the same as the entrepreneurial leadership model, and was discussed in Chapters 1 and 2. Before any entrepreneur or their salesperson goes on a sales call, in fact, before they even become an entrepreneur and/or salesperson, they have to understand themselves.

What does it take to become a motivated salesperson?

It takes insight into your makeup, into what you want, and knowing that you have the desire, commitment, and outlook to succeed.

We've all heard the 80/20 rule—you know, 80% of a company's sales are made by 20% of the salespeople in the organization. So, you really have to look inside yourself to see if you have the makeup to be part of that 20%. Otherwise, why waste your time?

It is vitally important to understand yourself so that you can be comfortable in your career. Once you understand who you are, not only in the part you play (e.g., salesperson, mother, father, softball player, book club member) but also in your intrinsic self, you begin to build self-esteem. Your self-esteem will grow as you achieve sales success for your business. You will begin to deal with the ups and downs of life in a more objective way.

With an understanding of the relationship between your "self" and your "part," it should be easier to begin to understand and categorize your goals.

Although all of us set goals of one type or another, those who put their goals in writing are more likely to achieve them. Writing your goals down often becomes a process of discovery. When you "see" the goals and objectives in a written form, it gets you to rethink what you wrote and you can prioritize them. People are more apt to refer back to their written goals. They are a documented record of where they want to go. That's why we've spent so much time throughout this book laying out the different types of goals you'll need to succeed. Whether the discussion is about vision, mission, strategy, action plans, or execution, having things in writing is extremely important.

So, how do you achieve your sales goals? Let's relate it to another question, "How do you eat an elephant?" And the famous answer, "One bite at a time!" Well, the same goes for sales. You can't get to the moon if you haven't built a spaceship. It's best to start with realistic goals and, as you achieve those, go on to the next. With diligence and perseverance, you'll see how things can expand and multiply. Before Neil Armstrong walked on the lunar surface, someone had to set the goal and lots of people had to work through the process.

Understanding Others

Once you have a clear picture of who you are, you can then learn how to interact successfully with others.

As we've mentioned, there's a saying that "People buy from people they like." For the most part, that's absolutely true. That doesn't mean that, if you need a bandage for a bleeding wound, you wouldn't buy it from a jerk. But if you were shopping for bandages just to have them in the house and the salesperson was indeed a jerk, then you would probably tell him or her to go pound sand and buy it from someone else. To paint an even more pointed scenario, if you had that bleeding wound and two salespersons were there to wait on you, one being the jerk and the other being a caring, compassionate individual, who would you give the sale to?

So, in the real world, it's how you interact with your prospect that helps give you the edge.

People buy emotionally. Needs, wants, distresses, frustrations, and other emotions push people to take action. It's those emotions that fuel the buying engine. This is where the power of listening—really listening and observing—comes in handy. These two skills make it easy to make the emotional connection you must make today to get the sale. Being able to uncover those emotions is key to becoming a successful entrepreneur, illustrating sales leadership, building a professional sales team, having a growing company, and being viewed by employees and customers as an entrepreneurial leader who listens.

There are three ingredients that entrepreneurs and sales professionals should understand. Knowing these "ABCs" will help in the uncovering process when interacting with prospects.

- Types of Attitudes
- Types of Behaviors
- Types of Communication styles

Attitudes are the reasons why individuals do things; it's what moves them into action. Attitudes are derived from our beliefs. Behaviors are the manifestations of how we do things. Communication styles are the tools we use, or don't use, in gathering, processing, and delivering information and ideas. Although we've talked about each of these items previously, we haven't related them specifically to the process of sales—the engine that will grow your company.

Knowing the different types of attitudes, behaviors, and communication styles of individuals can help in building rapport between you and your prospects and clients. Understand your core attitude, behavior, and communication style first. Then learn how to recognize and adapt to the attitudes, behaviors, and communication styles of your prospects and clients. Being adaptable will give you added control of the sales process.

Getting Prospects

For many entrepreneurs and salespeople, getting prospects means many things. In the beginning, getting prospects means cold calling, joining networking groups and organizations, and advertising. No matter what it is, every businessperson and/or salesperson needs to be able to easily and simply explain what he or she does without seeming like he or she is selling.

One technique is to pretend that you are advertising on TV or radio and have limited time to tell people who you are. Write a short and simple description of what you do without sounding like a salesperson and you're on your way. You can even use that self-description in your cold calling.

There are plenty of entrepreneurs and salespeople who make their living as a result of cold calls. For these people, every call is a means to an end. As an old friend once said, "The average sale I close is worth $2,000. I'll make 100 calls a day for 15 contacts to get two appointments that may result in one close. I'll take those odds every day of my life!" And he has done extremely well for himself. Of course, he doesn't have to make cold calls today because all those old cold-call clients have become very good referral sources for him. As he says, "It works!" So, looking at it from that angle, one thousand calls a month could put the cold caller on the road to doing quite well.

With a new perspective on the attitudes, behaviors, and communication styles of yourself and others, you can begin to see how your interaction with clients and prospects can cause them to feel good about you and what you're selling. As you begin to build rapport with clients and prospects, opportunities will begin to present themselves. You can get into a position to ask for (and get) referrals.

Referrals come when you have satisfactorily given your client or prospect what they wanted and more. People do things according to their own agenda. In other words, everyone is tuned into the same radio station WII-FM (What's In It For Me?).

You have to recognize and acknowledge your clients' and prospects' expectation levels. The more you do that, the easier it will become to make a sale. If you keep your clients and prospects happy, you can begin to build up a pool of credible personal and professional recommendation sources.

But to make people happy you have to have them as a client first!

Earlier, we spoke about buying a bandage for a bleeding wound. Sure, you'd buy it from the jerk if your blood was spilling on the floor, but you'd feel so much better buying it from the compassionate person who took your pain to heart.

Now suppose your wound wasn't visible to the salesperson, but the salesperson knew how to find out about it? What if he or she also enabled you to realize that you should do something about it? Wouldn't you be willing to buy something to get rid of your anguish?

Getting prospects and clients to buy is all about making them aware of their distress and, in some cases, their pleasures. Once you understand a person's distress, you begin to take control of the selling process.

How does someone find those distresses? The answer: by asking questions and listening to the answers. Potential customers will tell you everything you need to know if you just ask the right questions and listen to the responses. The 30% rule is one worth remembering and implementing: Successful salespeople know that they should only talk 30% of the time, at most. That leaves 70% for your prospect or client to tell you everything you need to know.

If you learn how to listen, the sales gates will open. There are certain questions that help you get the answers you need. Those answers will even tell you whether or not you have a "suspect" (someone who might or might not need your products or services) or a "prospect" (someone who might need your products or services) on your hands. Once you have ascertained that the suspect is not a prospect, you can continue to go on to the next person. You're better off knowing that someone is not a prospect at the beginning of the process than wasting time and finding it out later.

Making Agreements

Time and experience have taught us that if you don't have certain agreements lined up before you head into an appointment, you're probably wasting your time. Remember, you are as much a professional in your area as the person you are meeting. Just as they don't need to waste their time, you don't need to waste yours. Sales leaders and effective entrepreneurs realize that wasting time is a drain on their productivity and potential and actual revenues.

Agreements are the ground rules of your meetings and discussions. Remember, while you are setting up the ground rules and all through your meetings, you are using your knowledge of the ABCs of effective salespeople.

Make sure you set a time frame for your meeting. Find out what your prospect/client is hoping to get out of the meeting. Let them know what you are hoping to get out of the meeting. Put what you see as potential roadblocks, such as budgets, attendance of decision-makers, and relative price, on the table before the meeting begins.

By getting issues agreed upon before you meet, you and your prospect/client will save valuable time and energy. In addition, you will have learned more about your prospect/client than you would have if you dove headfirst into your meeting without asking questions and listening to those all-important answers.

Adding Value

As we've discussed, there is no reason to give prospects or clients your product or service knowledge until you understand what they need. By now, you may have realized that, by the prospect/client telling you their pertinent information, they may be closing the sale for you.

What you need to do at this point of the process is to give your prospect/client the information he or she has told you he or she needs. You can even ask them what they would like you to do. "If you were me, what would you do next?" is a question that evokes a great and telling answer.

You can see how much time and money you've saved by not giving away too much information, making needless extra qualifying or dequalifying meetings, or spending time tracking people down without knowing what they want.

Now is when you add your value by addressing the relevant points.

Long ago, you started to learn what they needed by asking, listening, using your ABCs, probing, and listening some more. Now, all you have to do is produce only those things that address the issues they've revealed. When you have been instructed by your prospect/client as to what he or she needs, you are in the final step to getting the sale.

Closing

Don't ever be afraid to ask for the order! Remember you are giving them the vehicle to do away with their problems. And don't ever be afraid to ask for payment. You sure would be willing to pay whatever it costs to get that bandage to stop the wound from bleeding that we discussed earlier, wouldn't you?

SOLID SALES SEQUENCE IS IMPORTANT

These six simple steps can help you build a much more successful sales career and grow your entrepreneurial venture in a more time-efficient manner. The order and integration of each step are extremely important. The foundation of the steps is the ABCs of communication. Without them, the other five steps would be much harder, if not impossible, to climb.

Solid sales success is attainable for salespeople in all professions. What they must do first is gain better control of their selling skills. Too often, salespeople feel that they're at a loss when entering a client's domain. It's not unusual for salespeople to say that they "just can't make this call, or the prospect already has a vendor, or the prospect's friend is taking care of that account, or I don't know, it just doesn't feel right," or any number of excuses.

Through listening, learning, understanding, and responding to their clients' needs, entrepreneurial leaders and/or sales professionals can gain the upper hand. Remember that sales should be a win-win situation for everyone. Clients, customers, and salespeople should always feel good about the sales process; otherwise, there's something wrong.

The sales process today is about building relationships. Effective entrepreneurial leaders know that real growth is based on customer satisfaction; following the tenet of making the customer feel good is one of the easiest ways to build an enterprise and be viewed as an industry leader. Satisfied customers will help you retain your current clients and gain new ones.

Becoming successful at sales may be about control, but it's not about manipulation, lack of caring, or taking advantage of anyone. Sales success is also about finding needs, fulfilling those needs, following up, representing honestly and correctly, adding value, and having fun. Although it's true that people buy emotionally, sales are sustained rationally. So look for distress, fear, concerns, weaknesses, and needs; provide solutions and solve problems, and you will create opportunities.

THE SIX STEPS TO SOLID SALES SUCCESS™ AND EMPLOYEES

Although The Six Steps to Solid Sales Success™ lay out a process for sales, they also work in dealing with your employees. Everyone is buying something, whether it's your leadership style, your ideas, or your vision, mission, strategy, or action plan. Your customers can be internal to your organization like your employees, partners, and other shareholders. Your customers can be external as well. Your external customers are not only those people who buy your products and services, but also can include stakeholders such as the surrounding community, governmental agencies, nonprofit organizations, your suppliers, the media, your distributors (if you use additional sales outlets), and, in some cases, the global community (this is becoming more and more evident as the Internet becomes increasingly pervasive).

CHANGE MANAGEMENT

As your enterprise changes, whether that change is self-generated or due to outside factors such as governmental regulations, new financial institution policies, competition, naturally occurring situations like climate change or unfortunate disasters, you will have to deal with the consequences. Learning how to listen, evaluate, respond, and sell your thoughts and ideas to others is the challenge of a real leader. Those who know the value of well-targeted sales skills can find the path of change much more manageable than those who either fight change or lack the ability to listen.

Change management is based on a clear understanding of who you are. Once again, understanding yourself and your ethical framework will be your adaptive guide as your business changes. Stephen Covey refers to this as your "changeless core." "People can't live with change if there's not a changeless core inside them. The key to the ability to change is a changeless sense of who you are, what you are about and what you value."

In today's fast-moving society, managing change is one of the most important skills an entrepreneur can acquire. The pace of innovation, globalization, and other factors that affect business is so incredibly fast that the entrepreneurial leaders who aren't thinking about tomorrow while planning for today may find themselves left at the starting gate.

When the U.S. automobile companies were slow to react to Japan's entrance into the market back in the 1970s, they lost such substantial percentages of customers that they never recovered. Their reaction to change was surprisingly slow, and they've paid the price for it ever since. If they had looked at the market with a broader, less-entrenched view, it's quite possible that the United States' economy and that of Japan and likely the economy of the rest of the world would look incredibly different today.

A prime example of rapid change management is the food industry. Not that long ago, Americans ate a "meat and potatoes" diet. Today's palates have quite a bit more choices. Sushi has become part of many Americans' daily intake; Vietnamese food, nouvelle cuisine, Russian delicacies, and so many other dishes from throughout the world are no longer oddities on the kitchen and restaurant tables of the United States. The change in many of America's desired foods is part of the globalization of commerce.

Entrepreneurial chefs have led the charge in this dietary change. Many others have followed suit—with fast food chains changing their menus at a rapid pace to keep up with the new habits of the American consumer. The pervasiveness of coffee shops is another example. Many restaurants, supermarkets, and convenience stores have had to install coffee bars, others have upgraded their selections, while still others have introduced new flavors as well as special teas. Those who adapt may survive and those who do not may become extinct.

Managing change means having your finger on the pulse of now and the future at the same time. Technology companies live by that principle. Today's software can be obsolete even before it hits the market. New computer-related products could have phenomenal sales cycles, generating amazing amounts of revenue within months, and, shortly thereafter, see the market share dwindle as a new product, sometimes by an unheard of competitor, appears on store shelves.

In the spring of 2007, Don faced a fundamental change in the mission of his team at the SBDC. The SBDC team had been recognized regionally and nationally for what it had accomplished with its e-Learning strategy. But that was yesterday. The environment had changed, and it needed to change as well. Instead of just providing tools, the SBDC needed to provide individualized consulting help to their clients. The center needed to meet with more clients and record more impact in a shorter period of time with fewer resources. To deal with the change, the SBDC team followed a process very similar to the Solid Sales process.

First, team members knew themselves. They were aware of their "changeless core," as Stephen Covey puts it. Second, they confirmed that the fundamental change was not in conflict with their vision. Once that was ensured, they next turned to their strategies. They looked at their strategies and determined if any of them could help make this fundamental change in their mission. Don notes that this was a moment of much soul searching and anxiety—typical ground in the territory of leadership. They determined that the e-Learning strategy was a perfect model for designing and developing a new e-Consulting strategy.

They set about creating a new consulting process based on the utilization of Internet technology. There was a steep learning curve for the entire team over the next six months. This period of team building went through the usual process of forming, storming, norming, and performing. The team had moments of frustration and anger and the usual ups and downs, a natural part of the change management process, but they fought through them and found their way to a new level of performance.

Don explains what they did. "We were looking to develop a cost-effective way to provide meaningful consulting to more entrepreneurs, an objective that hundreds of other organizations had tried with limited success. The answer, we saw, was staring us in the face—our successful Internet learning program would work if we applied it to the consulting process."

One of the remarkable aspects of this change management experience was rediscovering the power of the telephone. "Necessity is the mother of invention" and, in this case, they invented a viable solution. With a simple phone call to entrepreneurs registering for online learning programs, they nearly tripled the number of people attending Webinars. The change forced them to rethink everything they were doing. They even rethought how they used the mail. They integrated snail mail into the consulting process, and it became another touch point with clients. They now had a new mission aligned with their vision, ethics, and strategies.

The entrepreneurial leader spends time listening, training, taking classes, learning, networking, innovating, and anticipating. Lifelong learning is a continuum. The more one learns, the more one realizes that change is always happening. The trick is to know how to manage yourself so that you can more effectively manage others along with the change that is certain to come.

KEY POINTS AND LESSONS LEARNED

- ☑ Continuous learning is the fuel of growth and more profits.
- ☑ Change is the only constant in life.
- ☑ The Internet will be a major part of the future of every business.
- ☑ Learn and nurture your selling skills to be an effective leader.
- ☑ People buy from people they like and buy based on emotion.
- ☑ If you learn how to listen, the sales gates will open.
- ☑ Don't ever be afraid to ask for the order.
- ☑ Manage change by adapting for improvement but retain your "changeless core."
- ☑ Effective leaders manage themselves through continuous learning so they can better manage others.
- ☑ Individual growth is the underpinning of entrepreneurial leadership.

9

Success

My will shall shape the future. Whether I fail or succeed shall be no man's doing but my own. I am the force; I can clear any obstacle before me or I can be lost in the maze. My choice; my responsibility; win or lose, only I hold the key to my destiny.

—Elaine Maxwell

Well, friends, you have journeyed through the first eight of nine steps that we developed to guide you to success as an entrepreneurial leader.

Of course, there is one remaining, and it is an all-important step to climb. It is the step of success. All the understanding of one's self; recognition of what motivates you and where your ethical standards lie; how you see your vision, mission, and strategy; the paces you need to go through to complete and implement your action plan; what it takes to understand others so they can share your vision and values; how you will empower your employees and your business so they and it can grow; and what you need to do to keep yourself on track, growing, changing, learning, while you manage yourself toward success is the process that led you up to this point. As the entrepreneurial leader, you will shape the future of your business and you hold the key to your destiny.

Now is when you face the probability of success. Standing on the top of the pyramid means different things to different people. As you've noticed through the narratives and examples in this book, Dan and Don have experienced success in a variety of ways, as have the other entrepreneurs mentioned within their stories. What may mean success to you may have an entirely adverse meaning to someone else.

Hopefully, you've realized what success is for you by going through the exercises and stories in the previous chapters. When Dan began each of the businesses he discussed, his ultimate goal was to help others. If he was effective in reaching that objective, he felt satisfied. That measure of success may be different from yours, but it is still valid. Making boatloads of money could be your primary measure, or staying home while creating

Figure 9.1
The Leadership Model—Success

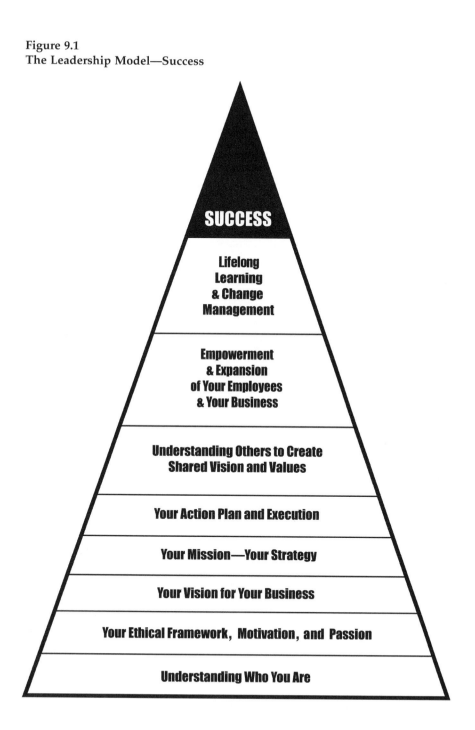

SUCCESS

Lifelong
Learning
& Change
Management

Empowerment
& Expansion
of Your Employees
& Your Business

Understanding Others to Create
Shared Vision and Values

Your Action Plan and Execution

Your Mission—Your Strategy

Your Vision for Your Business

Your Ethical Framework, Motivation, and Passion

Understanding Who You Are

a comfortable existence might be what you're striving for. Perhaps you want to travel, and monetary rewards are secondary, then walk yourself through the steps and go for it. Success, like beauty, is in the eye of the beholder.

However, once you reach the top, staying there may be difficult. Keeping up with the latest trends, information, predictions, regulations, employee situations, technological skills and programs, competitive environments, and other things that can make the peak a slippery slope is why we put it on a foundation that addresses all of these issues.

Every day, the entrepreneurial leader must walk up the steps to the point that signifies success. The leader knows that everything is temporary. Life itself is that way. So, just as success is sweet, it must be nurtured like a plant, watered, fed, cared for, and watched over. There is a reason that many of yesterday's success stories are today's failures: complacency. Fat, dumb, and happy is what some people might call it. The leader knows that when an organization becomes fat (which means too many layers of management, too much inventory, too many unnecessary locations, an overabundance of advertising, displays of self-righteousness, and any other indication that one has become blinded by one's own success), it is ripe for disaster. Of course, even if the company cruises along in the fat stage without sinking, the dumb stage could be the iceberg that may do it in. Dumb often translates into not paying attention to the surrounding environment. Frequently, the signs of change may be all around, but the dumb company may not notice them. As the organization floats happily along, direct competitors, new entrepreneurs, or other happenstances may quickly turn the happy stage into a very sad situation.

10-PART ENTREPRENEURIAL QUIZ

The 10-Part Entrepreneurial Quiz (see Figure 9.2) is designed to be taken by the entrepreneur, but it's even better if taken by your entire team as a group. It is helpful to take the quiz frequently, but especially any time you are looking to change your mission. The quiz can help your team stay grounded and laser focused on success and what got you there. It helps team members find the motivation and energy to continue at the success level.

Before you take the quiz, get together with your team. Scan the model with your minds and hearts. Take a moment to collect your thoughts. Reflect and appreciate all that you and your team have accomplished. Enjoy the feeling. This effort will get everyone in the right frame of mind to begin the process of working to move forward.

On the left side of the model, the first four components, we will revisit the foundational steps of the Leadership Model. On the right side of the model, in the last six components, we will drill down to how we have implemented the values, vision, and mission we defined. The final item is more of an action step than a question—just to ensure that we are keeping the customer at the top of our minds.

Figure 9.2
The 10-Part Entrepreneurial Quiz

Who Am I? Who Are We?

Now that you have arrived at the success level, the first thing to do is review the current understanding of yourself and, more important at this stage, who you have become. You have achieved a level of success based on building a dedicated team committed to your vision and mission. As we have said, hiring the first person was the most critical step to your success, and doing that helped facilitate the hiring of the next 100. Now you have a team, and the team must answer the question: "Who Are We?"

Mary Kay Ash was an entrepreneur who created a company with a vision of providing cosmetics to women through direct sales. Her mission was to empower women as salespeople, and success was exemplified by a pink Cadillac. She grew her company around the globe with her belief. Mary Kay said it this way: "People are definitely a company's greatest asset. It doesn't make any difference whether the product is cars or cosmetics. A company is only as good as the people it keeps."

Your Ethical Framework

It's time next to check in with your ethical framework. What are your core values and principles that are the bedrock of your actions? What is your "changeless core?" As you evaluate your current success and look to the future, your core values and principles will be the foundation for growth. Sergey Brin, vice president of technology of Google, cofounded a business that in a few short years grew to be a multibillion-dollar enterprise. From the outset, he made a firm commitment to an ethical framework that he articulated to his employees, customers, and Wall Street: *Don't Be Evil*. To Sergey, making a difference in the world is as important as the financial success of Google. He states that point this way: "Obviously everyone wants to be successful, but I want to be looked back on as being very innovative, very trusted and ethical and ultimately making a big difference in the world."

Your Vision When It Is Finished

Your vision has brought you success. It compelled you to act and got others to buy into your dream on a deadline. Of all the steps in our entrepreneurial leadership model, this is the most powerful. Now, you need to revisit the vision that you sought to create and the vision that your team helped you to achieve. Looking back from the success level, it is time to review that vision and to evaluate how close you are to fulfilling it and whether you need to redefine or expand the vision of your business.

The one thing we know for sure is there always will be unrelenting change in the marketplace. You and your team have achieved success. Congratulations! Take time to celebrate your success. A. C. Elliott describes the experience when we first know we have achieved our vision: "The person who works diligently toward a dream, and keeps his focus on the goal, will wake up some fine morning and realize that he has achieved what he has dreamed."

Your Business's Mission

You need to take another long hard, look at your business's mission and its execution at the success level. Having a single overriding objective of executing the mission of the business with excellence is essential in today's business climate. Excellence can and must be the standard for your business as you seek to remain "in the game." Your mission should be your single overriding objective as you play the game. This is the opportunity to redefine that mission or expand it based on the business environment. You must look at the trends in the marketplace, the economy, and where new opportunities lie. Dwight Eisenhower, president of the United States, gave a speech on April 2, 1957, in which he said: "We succeed only as we identify in life, or in war, or in anything else, a single overriding objective, and make all other considerations bend to that one objective."

One key to success is to be open to an opportunity that could dramatically increase sales and profits. Earlier in the book, we mentioned that while Don was managing the business at the General Motors facility, he seized an opportunity to do desktop publishing to produce job aids for General Motors. Think about what might be such an opportunity for you.

Now that we've revisited the foundational items of our success model, we need to focus more specifically on our reason for being in business—the customer.

Your Pitch and 30-Second Spot

At the success level, it's prudent to take a hard look at your marketing message, your 30-second sales spot, and your business pitch. The ever-increasing rate of change in the marketplace may have made your message obsolete. Based on the decisions you will be making at the success level with your vision and mission, a whole new marketing plan will need to be created. If there is a change, you will have the difficult decision of deciding what stays and what goes. That process comes with the territory. Seek the advice of your success team and take a long, hard look at your competitors. Work with your outside marketing communications person and with your team inside to agree on the new "look and feel" of your marketing message.

Your Promise or Guarantee to Customers

Your implied or written promise and/or your guarantee to your customers needs to be revisited. One of the keys to your current success has been the loyalty of your customers and their referrals of new customers who are seeking the same experience. By reevaluating your product or service guarantee, you may make changes that are reflective of current trends in the marketplace while adhering to your ethical framework and the company's vision and mission. The trick is to revitalize your offering but retain the reasons that your core customers are loyal to you and your company.

What Business Am I Really In?

You need to answer three questions: The first question is: *What business am I really in*? If we ask a photographer that question, her answer should not be, "I take pictures." A better answer might be, "I sell memories." That answer gets at the key issue—people buy based on emotion. They are buying a reminder of the dimple on a child's cheek and not a piece of paper. Thus, we must be customer centric and figure out the right answer to the question.

Next, our challenge to you is to pause and take a hard look at the history of your business and answer the second question: *How do customers perceive our business*? What service are you really providing? This means you must really think through and feel "their pain." A customer centric view will open new vistas of understanding. Then, ask the third question: *What do customers see as our "magic?"* We know you are a success; now make sure you have enough of the "magic" in the bottle to sustain that success for the long term.

What Does Success Look Like?

When you built your action plan and laid out your key goals and objectives for the business as well as writing out the vision for your business, you created measures that you can now use to judge success. (We will provide some illustrations of business success later in this chapter.) It is critically important that you have a firm handle on what constitutes success. One of the reasons you have arrived at this success level has been your determination to achieve your goals; another is your pursuit of excellence. In trying to get a handle on what success looks like, it's very important to go back to that original desire you had to be an entrepreneur. Mario Andretti, a world-famous racecar driver, exemplifies someone who is committed to excellence and who had a powerful desire to succeed. He said, "Desire is the key to motivation, but it's determination and commitment to an unrelenting pursuit of your goal—a commitment to excellence—that will enable you to attain the success you seek."

How Does the Business Operate?

At the success level, operating your business is based on achieving excellence. The constant pursuit of excellence in operating a business is your key to continued growth and prosperity. It is always advisable at the success level to take a very hard look at the cost of operating the business and employing all your personnel. The current cost of energy is forcing entrepreneurs across the globe to reevaluate all of their energy uses and to look for alternative energy sources. A second part of the drive toward excellence is to reevaluate all your work processes and improve them. This can be done by working directly with your employees, and it almost always provides cost savings and new efficiencies. One of the habits that successful entrepreneurs need to nurture and develop is approaching little things with a fervor for excellence. If we get the small things right in the business, it will lead directly to getting the big things right. Colin Powell, former Chairman of the Joint Chiefs of Staff during the Gulf War, put it this way: "If you are going to achieve excellence in big things, you develop the habit in little matters. Excellence is not an exception, it is a prevailing attitude." Pat Riley, an outstanding basketball coach in the NBA, gives us another view on achieving excellence. Pat puts it this way: "Excellence is the gradual result of always striving to do better."

Understand Your Customer First

This final step in our 10-Part Entrepreneurial Quiz is the one that will get you moving to the next level of success. In the end, the entrepreneurial leader needs to look at the customer's pain. The entrepreneurial leader needs to really dig deep into the fire, not just the smoke. This will take time and energy. It will also take a spirit of being open-minded to the current environment your customers find themselves.

We are living in a revolutionary time based on the Internet, the cost of energy, and the emergence of the "flat world" of business. Today is an exciting time to be in business. There are limitless opportunities and simultaneous complex problems that face the business owner. You should work with your success team and get their insights into what they see coming in the next months or the next several years. It is also the time that you must invest part of your most precious commodity—time—into lifelong learning. The quest you are on is to determine the long-term viability of your business enterprise.

Leadership is all about keeping ears, eyes, and all the other senses wide open. The lifelong learning and change management that we discussed in the last chapter is a great vehicle to help ensure ongoing success.

To remind you of your fundamentals, it might be helpful to look at the answers to the 10-Part Entrepreneurial Quiz every day. Tape them to your computer, keep them on your desk, hang them on your wall, or attach them to your door. Review the steps often and make sure that each one of them is covered as you make decisions. It's a great check and balance. Don't take your success for granted or your success won't always be there.

Back in the last years of the last century, the dot.com era was at full throttle. Companies were popping up like weeds, and people were more than eager to throw money at them. As we all know, most of those organizations were overnight successes but quickly became flashes in the pan. If they would have taken a bit more time and been a little more diligent in their research, most of the venture capital firms that invested millions in them would have figured out that the vast majority of the entities were not based upon solid foundations.

When Dan was the chairman of the oil-and-gas company, a corporation that was interested in partnering with his group approached him. Many phone calls were exchanged. Sizable stretches of time were spent in meetings analyzing the offers, and a conclusion was finally decided upon. He remembered the day in the early 1990s when he had to make a decision: move forward with the negotiations, or move on to the next group. His research had come to one startling conclusion about the company that wanted to work with them: he couldn't figure out what the company actually did. He rejected moving ahead with them.

In hindsight, it didn't affect the outcome of his venture. If they had invested, it may even have made him some money in the short term. However, his ethics, motivation, and passion told him something didn't match. Fortunately, the company did not become his partner. Dan rejected Enron long before anyone else realized that it was to become the epitome of corporate greed and fraud.

YOUR LEGACY

As you build your entrepreneurial leadership skills, one thing that every leader should think about is the legacy he or she would like to leave behind. Whether you're 19 (or younger) and just starting out or you are up in years and ready to begin a new phase, your legacy is how others will deem your success. Will Bill Gates solely be remembered as the man who drove Microsoft into the stratosphere of companies, or will he also be remembered as the humanitarian who strove to drive disease away from the children of third-world countries? Will Warren Buffet be forever the Berkshire Hathaway maven or will his charitable contributions overtake his iconic business profile?

To many Americans, Donald Trump epitomizes success. His face is everywhere. His television show was, at least for a while, on the minds and lips of a huge number of people. He seems to have his hand in just about every business imaginable, and they also all seem to bear his name. He has a brand of bottled water, a university, casinos, residences, and a slew of other ventures. But does he signify success to you? And if he does, to what would you attribute his success? What is his legacy in your mind? Has he made the world a better place? Or should that not matter? If he has, how has he? These are all questions that others may ask about you. In fact, you may be asking them of yourself.

Ponder if you will the case of Aaron Feuerstein. To some of you his name may be familiar, for others it may have no meaning at all. Mr. Feuerstein was the CEO and owner of Malden Mills, based in Lawrence, Massachusetts. Mr. Feuerstein's company manufactured fabrics such as Polartec™ and Polar-fleece™. These fabrics were used to help their wearers stay warm during winter's cold weather. His products were incorporated into clothing made for some of America's most familiar retailers, such as Lands' End and L.L. Bean. He was the third generation to run the business his family had founded.

In December 1995, his facility was destroyed by fire. He had many choices. He could rebuild, while his workers were forced to collect unemployment, send his production overseas or to another state, or abandon his business and move on with his life.

He chose the former but with a twist. Rather than create a situation where his employees would receive a fraction of their wages while his factory was being rebuilt, he decided to take a different approach. He continued to pay his approximately 3000 workers in full (including benefits) during the months it took to get his operation up and running again.

His impact on Lawrence and the towns that surround it are storied. Driven by his ethics, values, and faith, Mr. Feuerstein helped thousands, including his employees, their families, and the communities in which they reside. His deeds became magnified through the media; his story appeared on every major network's news program. He was interviewed on many TV magazine shows as well as in the print media.

His sensitivity to his workforce saved their economic lives, at least for a while. However, debt ravaged the company and eventually forced it into bankruptcy. Today, it exists in a different form, run by different people. Still, Aaron Feuerstein believes that what he did was the right thing to do, in the long term and the short term. His deeds dealt more with his value system than money, and his generosity has become legendary. Don had the pleasure of meeting Mr. Feuerstein and hearing his story a few years ago when he came to Kutztown University to speak about the fire and his response. He touched everyone that night. He was the businessman that we all, at times, long to be.

Would you consider Aaron Feuerstein a success? Would his actions be something that you would emulate? Would you think of him as a leader? For him, ethical behavior was never in question; it was what he was brought up to do. If it had been up to you, what would you have done in the same situation? It is an excellent exercise to ponder.

Much has been made of Aaron Feuerstein's charitable behavior. He has received many awards and accolades including the 2005 Stanley C. Pace Leadership in Ethics Award. His selflessness has been chronicled many times over. Even though he may have lost his company, he still thinks of himself as a success.

Needless to say, Aaron Feuerstein's employees stuck with him through thick and thin, as he did for them. People can sense authenticity; so, be authentic with all of your stakeholders and they'll be apt to stick with you during the down times as well as when times are good.

The impact you have on others—on your employees, family, and stakeholders—is something that puts you on the path to leadership and success. It's tough to recall any self-proclaimed leader who has withstood the test of time. To be a leader you must be hailed by others as a true leader. Your actions and how others see them will ultimately determine whether or not you have achieved becoming an entrepreneurial leader, which was our goal in writing this book.

Success, as we have seen, comes in many forms. Once you recognize your ability to fully understand the environment in which you play (remember that business is a game), then you'll have a clearer perspective of what it takes to win.

THE IMPORTANCE OF FUN

The lightness you emit also will play a significant role in your success. Making people want to work for you is an important element of successful leadership. Too much turnover can kill the most strategically well planned business, and it can create havoc during transition periods. Your commitment to your employees can help you retain valued workers and give your clients the image of a stable company.

Prior to opening For Eyes, Dan encountered a situation that could have derailed his new business before it began. How he handled it is something he discusses with his speaking and training audiences.

The story begins on the day that Dan had just begun his fabled dispensing (fitting eyeglasses) career in optics. He was nervous as he stood, well appointed, in his suit and tie. His short-haired wig was on just right (otherwise Dan's hair would have been flowing halfway down his back). This little older woman stood across from him, waiting anxiously for her glasses so that she could see perfectly again. Dan was too tense to ask her to sit down. He opened up her frames, grabbed her new glasses by the temples (side pieces), held them professionally between his thumb, index, and middle fingers and proceeded to place them on her face. As they were nearing her ears, Dan couldn't understand why they wouldn't go any further. He was struggling to set them on their proper resting place and be cool at the same time. Finally this very calm and kind woman (probably realizing that she was his first victim) said, "Look down, on my face, look down." There stuck in her nostrils were the nose pads, so perfectly inserted, pulling her nose upright and certainly not permitting those temples to rest on her ears!

Dan felt like an idiot. For that split second, he didn't know whether to get down on his knees and beg for her forgiveness or consider taking up a new profession in rhinoplasty (doing nose jobs). Fortunately, Ms. Nose

Pads began to laugh hysterically. Dan, relieved, caught the moment and began to howl. He felt fortunate.

Dan went on to build his own successful business, and the experience made him determined to keep fun in his organization.

An entrepreneurial leader should always be willing to laugh. The stimulation/fun factor is so important that it's one of the main reasons people leave one career to go on to the next. Another common reason to leave is lack of appreciation. Also remember always to recognize the well-done jobs of your coworkers.

Don't freak out when others make mistakes. Those things will happen, and the way you handle those tribulations will speak volumes to your workers, clients, vendors, family, as well as to your own nervous system and blood pressure. Of course, there is a process for dealing with mistakes. First you forgive the mistake. Then you can explain what should have been done in those situations. Give and receive feedback. Enable people to process the information and the mentoring you give them. Let them feel free to ask you anything about their job.

A caring approach usually gets a caring response. However, we always run the risk of folks who will take advantage of the good natured. Be aware of those who would do that. Don't be afraid to sit with those people and spell out the consequences of that type of behavior.

If business is a competitive game and you've chosen to participate, then we've got to get to the goal line before the opposition. There's nothing more fun than winning at a challenging game you've chosen to play.

An interesting side note to Dan's experience with Ms. Nose Pads is that she became a regular client of his and, when he opened his own business, she readily transferred her allegiance to Dan's new company and told all of her friends to do the same. Now that's turning a mistake into an opportunity.

PERFORMANCE: A KEY TO SUCCESS

Success and leadership come from performance. All the training, coaching, classes, and books are worthless unless you make the commitment to perform. How often have you left a training session all juiced up, ready to make a difference, until someone or something diverts you? Staying focused is such an important element of entrepreneurial leadership that it must be reinforced. We live in an environment that is continually bombarding us with more and more distractions that it's tough for the entrepreneur to hold firm. The leader will stay the course no matter what. Losing focus is a major reason that businesses fail. Success awaits those who keep it in their sights.

Have you ever had to make a deadline? Assuming that you have, you know that any and all interruptions become barriers to your ability to completing the task at hand. When you set out to become a successful entrepreneurial leader, look at each of our nine steps as tasks that you must complete to reach your goal.

Spend the necessary time to do self-reflection exercises. Think about your behavior, how you act and interact with others, understand yourself to the point where you can watch yourself and the reactions you create in others. Open up your filters and enable yourself to learn who you are as if you were viewing another person. It's a goal worth achieving because it is the basis for everything else you will strive for. An entrepreneur who can master the art of self-understanding is a leader in waiting. That entrepreneur is the one who will be able to adapt; that, in turn, will create the impetus for success.

SUMMARY

Know what lies deep inside you. By contemplating what moves you into action and why, you will have the keys to recognizing your ethical foundation, motivations, and passion. As you move forward toward and within your entrepreneurial endeavors, having a full comprehension of your ethical, motivational, and passion-driven aspirations will enable you to see your goals clearly. If the fire burns inside from a well-established place, it is less likely to extinguish at the first sign of trouble. Businesses derived from the elements we've listed in this paragraph are more likely to succeed because they are fueled by intrinsic desires. Stay focused on those factors and your chances of success are greatly enhanced.

Putting your vision into words will help you visualize what you want to do. It is the cornerstone of your business. Everything else revolves around your vision. Just like a cornerstone holds an arch together, your vision will be the anchor of your business. From your vision statement you will be able to derive the tasks that need to be done to achieve the success it holds out. Using its guiding words to help you decide your business's future will keep you focused on that end. A business without a vision is like a boat without a rudder; you may be able to see the shore but it will be difficult to get there through the squalls, winds, and other elements that lie before you.

Once you have your vision tightly woven into your entrepreneurial brain, you can move on to how you will achieve that sight through your mission and strategy. Seeing what to strive for through your vision, you must now set mind to machine and figure out what you intend to accomplish when reaching for your vision. Your mission will set those thoughts into a workable paragraph that should guide you along the path toward your goal. The strategy you establish will be the road map that will help guide you to where you want to be in the most effective way possible. The strategy, mission, and vision should all fit together seamlessly so as to make sense to you and anyone you may approach to become involved in your business.

With the fabric of your enterprise firmly in place, your action plan becomes the tactical side of your business's growth process. Laying a solid groundwork of actions to move your business along is like adding muscles to a skeleton. Your actions will now be able to speak louder than your words. They will set in place all the things that you will have to do to get you where you want to be. Executing those actions is the fuel that drives you down the road to success. Think of your action plan as an automobile. You have put all the pieces in place, but, to get it moving, you will still have to put fuel in the tank. Your ability to execute is that fuel. The most high-powered car in the world can go nowhere unless someone gets its pistons moving.

Now, everything that you want to set in motion is ready to go. You can see your vision becoming a reality, your mission and strategy are laid out before you, all the actions are spelled out as well, and you even have fuel in the tank. But you have to convince the crew that not only do you want to get your car rolling down the highway, but also you want them to be passengers along with you. Learning how to understand others will help you know what it is that will motivate them to open the doors of your vehicle and get inside. By learning their motivators, you can then have them join you on their terms. Now that you know what things turn them on, you can present your vision, mission, strategy, action plan, and execution in terms that will enable them to buy in. If you recognize the importance of this step, you should have a car full of people at all times.

After a while you may no longer feel like driving. In fact, your passengers may even ask you for the opportunity to drive. If that's the case, you know that you've succeeded in getting a bunch of folks who not only understand where you are going, but also want to help you get there as well. By allowing others to drive, you have given them the power to move toward your goals for you while moving toward the same goals for themselves. They may even recognize the need for a trailer so that you can haul more things or get more people on board. Their thoughts may create new elements that you hadn't conceived of. Before you know it, you just might have a larger, faster, more efficient automobile moving toward success at amazing speeds.

With your bigger, more efficient, faster vehicle driving toward your objective, you may want to add even more gizmos to your trip through the world of entrepreneurial leadership. You know that there are new things out there that can help you, but you're not exactly sure what they are. All of a sudden you see a sign that says, "New gizmos to help your business grow, next left." Everyone decides that it might be a good idea to find out what those gizmos are so you make the next left and there, off on the right, is a building with a sign that says, "We can make your business life easier." You park, all pile out (even from the trailer), and go inside to find a person telling a room of people about something that will indeed help your business boom. You and your crew stay until the lecture is over, you buy the gizmo and leave. Everyone agrees that for the business to keep growing you should always look for ways to learn. And off you all go with your new GPS system toward success.

Finally, you are all where you want to be, you've made it to your destination. People are lined up waiting for you. Each person is ready to give you money, so that you can give him or her what it is that you set out to sell. You open your trunk and start to allow your customers to buy. Noticing that you'll quickly run out of product, you empty the trunk and tell some of your helpers to drive back and pick up more "stuff." You're business is succeeding, but you know that to keep it that way you have to keep learning, watch out for competitors (other cars coming down the road), make sure you're aware of the trends that may occur (cars with much bigger trunks), stay alert for new information (speed limits), predictions (different types of engines), regulations (the need for insurance), employee situations (backseat drivers), and technological skills and programs (fancy gizmos and more fancy gizmos).

As you progress down the road to success, you will encounter new and unexpected things. If you keep your mind open and your senses aware, then your chances of being blindsided can be minimized. Remember what we said earlier in this chapter; success is a slippery slope, but, if you have the right equipment with you, it can help prevent the type of slippage that could move you off the peak. Being two steps ahead, while everyone else is trying to stay one step ahead, will help ensure that your slope will never be so slippery that you can't stand on it with arms held high and say, "I've led my entrepreneurial endeavor to success!"

KEY POINTS AND LESSONS LEARNED

- ☑ You define success and are totally responsible for achieving it.
- ☑ Avoid complacency! Success contains the seeds of failure.
- ☑ Take the 10-Part Entrepreneurial Quiz to keep success in focus.
- ☑ Keep perspective of who you are and defend your ethical values.
- ☑ Know if you have attained your vision and if you should change your mission.
- ☑ Keep up with changes in the marketplace—technology and competitors.
- ☑ Hold on to your loyal customers.
- ☑ Define your legacy.
- ☑ Remember the Malden Mills story. Do what is right for your employees and customers.
- ☑ Keep fun in your organization.

Appendices

APPENDIX A: LEARNING RESOURCES

Introduction

Websites

Http://www.sba.gov. This is the most visited government site for small business. It will give you access to a large collection of free online training, access to local resources, and tools. Most important, you will get information on Small Business Administration (SBA) Loan Programs. This is a good starting point for all entrepreneurial leaders.

Http://www.sba.gov/aboutsba/sbaprograms/sbdc/index.html. Small Business Development Centers (SBDCs) provide management assistance to existing business and startups. SBDCs provide free, confidential consulting and low-cost educational programs. More than 1,000 SBDCs are located throughout the United States. You should contact your local SBDC and arrange for an appointment to discuss its services. One of the keys to entrepreneurial success is having an advisor or mentor for your enterprise.

Http://www.score.org. SCORE counselors to America's small business provide free, confidential counseling and training. SCORE volunteers share their wisdom and business experience. SCORE volunteers are frequently retired business executives. You should contact your local SCORE chapter and arrange to meet to discuss the services it can provide you. Our experience with SCORE has been very positive. The key to making the service productive is to locate a SCORE volunteer who has the skills and experience in an area of interest. We had a very successful relationship with the SCORE counselor who helped us with a pricing strategy.

Magazines

Fast Company. Fast Company is for the entrepreneurial minded who want to grow and lead their enterprise. *Fast Company* gets you thinking and gets the creative gears of your mind moving. This magazine publishes fascinating stories and has a very contemporary look and feel.

Inc., handbook of the American entrepreneur. In each issue, *Inc.* magazine will give you access to success stories and the latest thinking on management and leadership. You can expect to find features on sales and marketing, finance, management, and technology. A leader needs to be current with business trends—*Inc.* will help you.

Books

Johnson, Dr. Spencer, *Who Moved My Cheese?* G.P. Putnam, 1998. As you move to become an entrepreneurial leader, you will face the issue of change. *Who Moved My Cheese?* is already a classic bestseller and addresses the issue of change. Many fans and critics say the book is so easy to read—so simple. The power of the book as an entrepreneurial leader is how you interpret it and apply it in your role as business leader.

Kawasaki, Guy, *The Art of the Start*, Portfolio, 2004. The time-tested, battle-hardened guide for anyone starting anything is a must read for the entrepreneurial leader. Kawasaki's approach of having the entrepreneur build a 10-slide pitch is brilliant. It forces you to capture the essence and passion of your business using 30-point font and allowing only 20 minutes for you to do your presentation. The pitch process is critical at the startup, but it will have greater impact as you grow your business. Once you have written your pitch you can integrate it into all of your marketing materials and your Website. It will assist you with the sales process and all aspects of your marketing.

Chapter 1

Magazines

Fortune. In each issue of *Fortune* magazine, you will get access to information on big business, global economics, and insights into the global business environment. As an entrepreneur, it is critical as you lead your enterprise that you keep current with the major trends of business in your region and, ultimately, the trends worldwide in this new global economy. You can discover trends that could help you to move your enterprise in a new direction and find new opportunities. An example is the current trend toward green solutions, alternative fuels, and environmentally safe products.

Websites

Http://www.keirsey.com. This site will provide you the opportunity to take an assessment instrument, called "Temperament Sorter." This online questionnaire will take you ten minutes to complete and will give you a free assessment of your temperament. It is very important for a leader to understand his or her temperament. The instrument will compare you to people with similar temperaments and tell you the vocations that they have selected.

www.msn.com. This site will give you access to current financial news and national news. In addition, you can get up-to-the-minute reports on the stock markets. As an entrepreneurial leader, it is critical to keep up with the current trends on Wall Street because they have a tremendous impact on what happens on Main Street. You should always be able to comment on current business and financial trends and be in a position to ask your key advisors about the potential impact on your business.

Books

Covey, Stephen R. *The 7 Habits of Highly Effective People*. Simon & Schuster, 1989. This book is a classic in providing powerful lessons in personal change. As an entrepreneurial leader, you will find the author's integrated approach for solving business problems and personal problems very helpful. The book gives you the opportunity to explore yourself and the impact that you have on those in your business, and it can help you to build new, more powerful relationships with the people in your circle of influence.

Isay, David. *Listening Is an Act of Love*. Penguin Press, 2007. *Listening Is an Act of Love* will give you insights into the most important communication skill you need as an entrepreneurial leader: listening. There are powerful stories all around you. All you need to do is to take time to listen. This book is the outcome of the StoryCorps project of National Public Radio (NPR), which created an opportunity for people to come together in a recording studio and share part of their life's story. Successful entrepreneurial leaders demonstrate on a daily basis the art of listening and empathizing with the speaker.

Chapter 2

Magazines

Business Week. Entrepreneurial leaders need to select one or two business magazines that they will regularly read. *Business Week* has remained one of the magazines that businesspeople turn to on a regular basis. It gives you an overview of what's going on from a national and international standpoint. It has a section for small business on its Website that is worth a regular visit. (You can find that Website at: www.businessweek.com/smallbiz/.)

Websites

Http://www.en.wikipedia.org/wiki/Business_ethics. Wikipedia is an online encyclopedia with over two million articles that was started in 2001. You will have access to information on all business topics. Spend some time on this site and you will find it to be of help. It's growing every day and adding more articles of business interest.

Http://www.instituteforethicalawareness.org. The Institute for Ethical Awareness's Website will give you access to articles, opinions, and research on ethical issues. As a business leader you should take some time to be familiar with ethical issues. The home page provides you with an illustration of unethical behavior and its potential consequences. The illustration also outlines how unethical behavior affects the initiator and those subjected to his or her behavior.

Http://www.willitfly.com. Willitfly.com is a modular knowledge base that allows you to look at best practices in the area of small business. In addition, willitfly.com asks you diagnostic questions and then prescribes educational briefs for your reading. It has over 8,000 diagnostic questions and some 1,400 educational briefs covering all of the business tasks that face the entrepreneur. You will find many of the educational briefs a great help to you.

Books

Gerber, Michael. *The E-Myth Revisited.* HarperCollins, 1995. This book is a must read for the entrepreneurial leader. It provides powerful lessons on owning and running a small business. The book confronts the issue that understanding the technical work of the business is not enough for business success. Gerber walks you through the lifecycle of most small businesses and provides insights and concrete steps that you can utilize in your business.

Chapter 3

Websites

Http://www.entrepreneurs-journey.com/724/do-you-lack-a-powerful-vison/. This Website is unique in that the entrepreneur in charge is from Australia—down under. It has a blog and some well-written articles that can give you a head start on developing your entrepreneurial leadership skills. The link above will take you to an article focused on building a powerful vision.

Http://www.eventuring.kauffman.org/. This Website is an essential resource for all small business owners. The site is funded by the Ewing Marion Kauffman Foundation in Kansas City. The Kauffman Foundation is the largest entity in the world dedicated to helping entrepreneurs. You will find articles on critical items related to entrepreneurship. In addition, the Kauffman Foundation does extensive research on entrepreneurial issues.

Http://www.mindtools.com. We recommend this Website and strongly suggest that you look at this powerful approach to note taking. We have used this approach throughout our entrepreneurial endeavors. It is listed in this chapter because we have utilized the technique in creating vision statements for various enterprises. The technique, popularized by Tony Buzan, is called "Mind Mapping." By using Mind Mapping, you can build a two-dimensional picture on one page instead of on ten pages. We like the technique because we can incorporate into our Mind Map all the key leadership issues, such as our ethical framework and who we are. This Website will give you examples of Mind Maps, and you will see how easy it is to get started using this process. We use Mind Maps with staff meetings (internally) and we have used it with clients (externally) as a way of building a strong communication among meeting participants.

Http://www.quickmba.com. This Website will give you insights into building your vision and your mission statements. It will review the building of your core values (ethical framework), the purpose of the business, and what they term "visionary goals" for the business.

Books

Pink, Daniel H. *A Whole New Mind*. Berkley Publishing Group, 2005. This book has become a resource for entrepreneurs who are trying to decide what will or will not be outsourced. Daniel Pink takes you through his concept of why right-brained thinkers will be able to flourish in a business environment that is increasingly finding American jobs and processes being sent abroad. This is a must read for anyone who wants to stay ahead of the curve.

Renehan, Jr., Edward J. *The Lion's Pride: Theodore Roosevelt and His Family in Peace and War*. Oxford University Press, 1998. Entrepreneurial leaders need to model the behavior that they want from their employees. In addition, they need to inspire, motivate, and demonstrate passion for their enterprise. Reading biographies can help you in becoming a more effective leader. We strongly suggest that you look at biographies of prominent Americans. Theodore Roosevelt overcame childhood illnesses and tackled life head on. He is inspirational, dynamic, and, most importantly, he became the leader in the 20th century who redrew the definition of the president. When we look back on his accomplishments, we recognize that he is one of our top ten presidents.

Wood, Gordon S. *The Americanization of Benjamin Franklin*. Penguin Press, 2004. This Pulitzer Prize winner is a superb read. Benjamin Franklin was one of our founding fathers and clearly the most entrepreneurial. Franklin was a visionary and a creative genius who brought to us a myriad of things. We can learn from Franklin about leading our businesses. He was able to integrate his vision with his mission, and the book shows us how he did it. There are many failed visionary leaders just as there are failed leaders who focused only on their mission. Franklin combined both and created entrepreneurial success as well as being one of the most important historical figures of the American Revolution.

Chapter 4

Websites

Http://www.bizfilings.com. This site will give you information on the proper legal structure for your company. We strongly recommend the site as a source of information on creating your legal structure. They have a number of articles and a good FAQs (Frequently Asked Questions) section.

We strongly recommend that you have an attorney in your local area as part of your Success Team.

Http://www.census.gov/pub/epcd/www/naics.html. This Website will give you access to valuable market research information based on the North American Industry Classification System (NAICS). The NAICS coding system replaced SIC Codes on October 1, 2000. It categorizes and classifies a company's products and services and defines the size of a company (large or small). Service companies are classified by sales per year and manufacturing companies are classified by number of employees (typically). Having recent statistical data on your competitors can help you as you refine or modify your business mission.

Http://www.kutztownsbdc.org. The Kutztown University Small Business Development Center's Website is worth visiting. It will give you access to one of the largest collections of free online learning modules in the United States. The online module and tools will help you build business plans and strategic plans. There are courses on all functional areas of a business. We strongly recommend that you take the Accounting 101 module, Marketing 101, and the legal course. This will help you communicate with your Success Team.

Http://www.lifefdn.org. This Website will provide you with information on all forms of insurance. It was created by the Life and Health Insurance Foundation for education. The intention is to provide you with a one-stop resource for information about insurance. Most studies show that insurance is becoming one of the top two or three items that a business leader has to deal with every day.

Http://www.myownbusiness.org. This Website provides a great deal of information on accounting and bookkeeping. It will give you insights into your requirements for accounting services. We recommend that you retain a local accountant as part of your Success Team and that you use one of the accounting software packages to manage that function of your business.

Books

Adams, Bob. *Adams Streetwise Small Business Start-Up*. Adams Media Corporation, 1996. This national bestseller gives you a comprehensive outline for starting and managing your business. From marketing your business, to selling your products, to buying your office furniture, Bob Adams walks you through the process in short, to-the-point chapters that contain extensive illustrations. This easy-to-follow reference guide is a great book to have on your shelf.

Friedman, Thomas L. *The World Is Flat: A Brief History of the Twenty-first Century*. Farrar, Straus and Giroux, 2005. Thomas L. Friedman's work is one of the most important books that an entrepreneurial leader can read today. It was a best-seller and continues to be talked about. What he did was to review the wonders that have occurred since the 1980s that have completely altered how we do business today, when we do business, and where we do business. The world is truly flat in the age of the World Wide Web. We have seen the emergence of India and China as world economic powers. This occurrence has led to the creation of a middle class in both countries as well as in Russia. The book gives insight into the critical innovations in software and the evolution of the Internet and how they have completely revolutionized our world. Leaders must "run" faster and smarter in this new global economy.

Peters, Thomas J. and Waterman, Robert H. *In Search of Excellence.* HarperCollins, 1982. Tom Peters was voted as the second most influential leadership professional by Gurus International in an independent Internet study in 2007. He became a best-selling author in 1982 with his book *In Search of Excellence.* The book remains one of the top-selling business books of all time. It gives entrepreneurial leaders great insights into how they can move their company to become a problem-solving enterprise with as little business process overhead as possible. Peters and Waterman discuss eight themes of business that account for excellence. The book started as a research project focused on business organizations and what made them work well. Peters became a disciple of empowerment and decision making possibility at all levels of a company. We recommend all of Tom Peters' books as your leadership information base.

Chapter 5

Websites

Http://www.managementhelp.org. This is a comprehensive site that will help you with all aspects of planning. With a vast library of resources that include examples, templates, and other tools to help you formulate and write your plans, managementhelp.org is an extremely helpful site for any entrepreneur who is looking to put his or her thoughts on paper or in computers.

Http://www.sbdcnet.org. This is the national clearinghouse for the U.S. network of the Small Business Development Centers. As you build your action plan, you will find many of the links on this site very helpful. For instance, you will have access to a large number of completed business plans, and information on marketing and human resources that will be helpful during the action planning process.

Books

McGartland, Grace. *Thunderbolt Thinking.* Bard Press, 2000. A fun and innovative way to get you to think creatively, this book combines facts, exercises, cartoons, and strategies to help guide you along the path toward new and exciting ideas for your business. Grace McGartland's words will enable you to get those cobwebs out of your mind and unlock breakthrough thoughts that can lead to new products, processes, and services for you and your organization.

Chapter 6

Websites

Http://www.abetterworkplace.com. Part of the process of understanding others to create a shared vision and shared values for your company is to create "a better workplace." This Website provides you with resources and tools that will allow you to build people skills with your team. In addition, you will find information on team building and tools for collaboration. Finally, there is information on leadership development that you will find helpful.

Http://www.asaecenter.org. This site houses The American Society of Association Executives and The Center for Association Leadership. Here is an invaluable amount of information on how people within the same industries deal with issues and formulate policies and procedures, including how they create a shared vision for their organization. You should be able to gain tremendous insights into how others within your industry function by using the information on this site.

Books

McFarland, Lynne Joy, Senn, Larry E., and Childress, John R. *21st Century Leadership*. Leadership Press, 1993. If you would like to know what 100 of the top leaders in the United States think about leadership, then this is the book for you. The text is broken into chapters that address different aspects of leadership. Each subject is outlined and then followed by relevant interviews with various leaders who express their thoughts on the topic. You're sure to find some usable leadership gems within the pages of this volume.

Rapaille, Clotaire. *The Culture Code*. Broadway Books, 2006. This book will help you understand how different cultures view the same products and services. By giving you insights into how various constituencies characterize their own particular consumerist culture, as well as those of other countries, it brings to light why marketing can have such a varied impact depending on the audience. Clotaire Rapaille's experiences and stories, garnered from working with some of the world's largest corporations, will give you insights into new ways of selling what you produce.

Chapter 7

Websites

Http://www.asq.org. The American Society for Quality is an organization that promotes employee empowerment so that its members can provide quality goods and services for their customers. This site will enable you to see how other ventures empower their people so that they can grow and prosper. There is a vast array of information that can help you and your company build a culture of employee empowerment.

Http://www.wisegeek.com. This Website offers you access to some powerful articles on empowerment. The link to an excellent article on employee empowerment is http://www.wisegeek.com/what-is-employee-empowerment.htm. This site contains thousands of articles that would be of interest to an entrepreneurial leader.

Books

Blanchard, Kenneth, Zigarmi, Patricia, and Zigarmi, Drea. *Leadership and the One Minute Manager: Increasing Effectiveness Through Situational Leadership.* William Morrow and Company, Inc., 1985. Kenneth Blanchard has made a "franchise" out of his *One Minute Manager* books. You will find this short, easy-to-read book can provide some quick tips on personalized leadership that will help you get the best performance out of your staff. We have included this book in our Learning Resources because it focuses on situational leadership. As your business grows, it will become more important for you to exercise good situational leadership.

Ries, Al and Ries, Laura. *The Fall of Advertising and the Rise of PR.* Harper Business, 2002. In this new millennium, one of the keys to the success of small businesses is understanding the transition from an advertising-based marketing strategy to a public relations–based strategy. With the costs of advertising in newspapers, magazines, radio, cable, and TV ever increasing and less effective, a new strategy needed to emerge. What emerged was a strategy based on clients telling your story and the entrepreneur figuring out how to get that story into the media. The bottom line—you have to spend time and energy to increase your profile in the region your business operates in.

Chapter 8

Websites

Http://www.changingminds.org. This is an excellent site to learn the skills behind how to change people's minds and deal with the broader aspects of change management. There are numerous categories from which to choose, and each one addresses a different area of business and life. By reading through some of the articles and other forms of information you will gain valuable and usable insights while continuing your own personal learning and growth process.

Http://www.ngm.nationalgeographic.com/ngm/. *National Geographic* has an exciting Website to visit on a periodic basis. It really helps you get insights on global issues. Please refer to the write-up below.

Http://www.time.com. *Time* magazine's online magazine provides you with the news of the day, analysis from nationally known writers, access to multi-media and blogs. Please refer to the write-up on the next page.

Magazines

National Geographic. *National Geographic* has been around for over 100 years. In this new century, *National Geographic* has built a powerful Website, cable TV station, and magazine. We have included *National Geographic* magazine in the Lifelong Learning step of the Entrepreneur's Leadership Model because it provides insight into global trends such as global warming, the emergence of China and its super economy, as well as insights into other cultures. Part of entrepreneurial lifelong learning is keeping abreast of the environment to adjust the mission of the business. An example would be a company's response to $4.00 or $5.00 per gallon gasoline.

Time. Time magazine has been around for generations. It is critical for the entrepreneurial leader to be current with the news of the day. *Time* offers you the opportunity to get your news online as well as through a magazine. Many entrepreneurs still prefer to get their news in a magazine format versus reading on the Web. A weekly periodical such as *Time* gives you a snapshot of national and international events that can directly affect your business. The cost of magazines is miniscule today. Take advantage of a quick read that can help you to remain current.

Chapter 9

Websites

Http://www.dangoldberg.com. Dan's site contains articles, blogs, videos, audios, podcasts, online learning resources, and other valuable elements to help keep you updated, involved, and informed. You can sign up for his newsletter, receive his podcasts, take courses, and interact with others. The site is refreshed constantly and enables you to be in touch with Dan, Don, and Bud Batcher. We will have available a series of Webinars based on this book that will assist the business owner in implementing an entrepreneurial leadership model. The user friendly format helps as well. This is a great way to monitor your progress through the site's various tools and to also know where Don, Dan, and Bud will be appearing next.

Magazines

Wired. This year marks the 15th anniversary of *Wired* magazine. The past 15 years have seen a revolution in technology. We are in the information age, driven by the Internet. As we discussed in the book, you must have a Webmaster as part of your success team. Also, you must look to utilizing technology in the face of high energy costs. *Wired* gives you insights and opinions into the current technology and a glimpse of what's coming down the pike. Technology will not make your company great; it's only a powerful tool that the leader can use to achieve greatness in the enterprise.

Books

Collins, Jim. *Good to Great*. Harper Business, 2001. Now that you have arrived at the success level, Jim Collins' book, *Good to Great*, can help you discover some principles that will help you get to that next level. Collins' team selected two sets of comparison companies to study. What he wanted to find out was what transitioned companies to the highest level of performance. One of his discoveries was something we addressed in this book—good to great companies pay little attention to managing change or motivating people. Under an entrepreneurial leader as we have discussed, these situations are naturally taken care of. Please take a few minutes to check out his Website, www.JimCollins.com.

Goldberg, Dan. *Lighten Up and Lead*. AuthorHouse, 2007. Dan brings a whole new approach to leadership in this volume. He guides you through the process of how to have fun with customers and employees in order to help your business grow. This book provides illustrations, lessons, and real-life examples to help you understand the techniques needed to become an enlightened leader and empowers you with practical ways to use them. Written in an easy-to-read format, you will find yourself laughing, learning, and reflecting on new ways to grow your leadership abilities. This was the first collaborative effort of The Institute For Effective Leadership with the intention of helping the small business owner.

Key Words and Phrases

One hundred thirty words and phrases that the entrepreneur needs to incorporate into their vocabulary.

Words

Achievement	Delegation
Advantage	Demographics
Advertising	Discipline
Ambition	Dream
Anchoring	Driven
Assumption	Education
Attitude	Effective
Bargaining	Efficiency
Believe	Emotion
Benefits	Empowerment
Brand	Encourage
Challenge	Enlightened
Change	Entrepreneur
Communication	Ethics
Competency	Excitement
Competition	Execution
Concept	Experience
Confidence	Feelings
Consequence	Forecast
Curiosity	Goals
Dare	Growth

Guide

Humor

Implement

Independence

Initiative

Innovation

Inspiration

Integrity

Laugh

Leadership

Legacy

Leverage

Lifestyle

Listen

Management

Marketing

Mission

Motivation

Objectives

Partnership

Passion

Penetrate

Perception

Persistence

Pitch

Positioning

Publicity

Quality

Rainmaker

Rapport

Sales

Stakeholders

Strategy

Success

Team

Teamwork

Trust

Values

Vision

Vulnerability

Phrases

Adult Learning

Business Model

Business Plan

Core Values

Change Management

Circle of Influence

Client Satisfaction

Controlling Growth

Customer Service

Decision Point

Ethical Framework

Fiscal Responsibility

Key Metrics

Learning Resources

Lifelong Learning

Lighten Up and Lead

Management Team

Marketshare

Model Behavior

Performance Appraisal

Return on Investment

Schedule Management

Setting Goals

Shared Vision

Solving Problems

Team Building

The World is Flat

Time Management

Value Proposition

Win/Win

Underlying Magic

APPENDIX B: OUR TOP 17 RECOMMENDED BOOKS

1. *Lighten Up and Lead*, Dan Goldberg, AuthorHouse, 2007.
2. *Listening Is an Act of Love*, Dave Isay, Penguin Press, 2007.
3. *The Culture Code*, Clotaire Rapaille, Broadway Books, 2006.
4. *A Whole New Mind*, Daniel H. Pink, Berkley Publishing Group, 2005.

5. *The World Is Flat*, Thomas L. Friedman, Farrar, Straus and Giroux, 2005.
6. *The Art of Start*, Guy Kawaski; by Portfolio a member of The Penguin Group (USA), Inc., 2004.
7. *The Fall of Advertising and the Rise of PR*, Al Ries and Laura Ries, Harper Business, 2002.
8. *Who Moved My Cheese?*, Spencer Johnson, M.D., G.P. Putnam, 2002.
9. *Good to Great*, Jim Collins, Harper Business, 2001.
10. *Thunderbolt Thinking*, Grace McGartland, Bard Press, 2000.
11. *Adams Streetwise Small Business Start-Up*, Bob Adams, Adams Media Corporation, 1996.
12. *The E-Myth Revisited*, Michael E. Gerber, Harper Business, 1995.
13. *21st Century Leadership*, Lynne Joy McFarland, Larry E. Senn, John R. Childress, Leadership Press, 1993.
14. *Truman*, David McCullough, Simon & Schuster, 1992.
15. *The Seven Habits of Highly Effective People*, Stephen R. Covey, Simon & Schuster, 1989.
16. *Leadership and the One Minute Manager*, Kenneth Blanchard, Patricia Zigarmi, Drea Zigarmi, William Morrow and Company, Inc., 1985.
17. *In Search of Excellence*, Thomas J. Peters, Robert H. Waterman, Jr., HarperCollins, 1984.

Index

About the Authors

DAN GOLDBERG is a trainer, coach, keynote speaker, entrepreneur, and marketer. Founder and former owner of the For Eyes optical chain, he has been featured in *Newsweek, Business Week, Investor's Business Daily,* and many other publications. He is Adjunct Professor at the Fox School of Business, Temple University; a Director and Senior Fellow at the Institute for Effective Leadership; and President of Dan Goldberg Consulting, L.L.C.

DON MARTIN is a trainer, mentor, business developer, and master salesman. He founded Learning Resources Technical Training, Inc., and PICE, Inc. He is Program Manager of Learning Resources for the Kutztown Small Business Development Center in Pennsylvania, and a Director and Senior Fellow at the Institute for Effective Leadership.